More TYBEE ISLAND

HEROES AND HOOLIGANS

The Making of an Island Paradise, Vol. 2

J.R. Roseberry

Cover Art: The cover photo, taken by J.R. Roseberry, shows noted Savannah adventurer and artist Albert Seidl rendering a painting of Tybee's historic lighthouse in the late 1990s, prior to the changing of it's "daymark" and renovation under the auspices of Cullen Chambers (see Chapter 4). Albert, who was one of the featured "Heroes" in Volume One, passed away on May 3, 2019. The caricatures below the photograph are of the characters included in this book. They were created by Mallory Pearce (see Chapter 17). Back cover photo by Lauren Clackum. Author photo by Ben Goggins.

Paperback ISBN: 978-1-959563-08-2
Hardback ISBN: 978-1-959563-09-9
eBook ISBN: 978-1-959563-10-5

Published by:
Maudlin Pond Press
P.O. Box 53
Tybee Island, GA 31328
www.maudlinpond.com

Photo of M. Louise Truxal from the S.M.S. 1953 Yearbook "The Castellan."

Dedicated to M. Louise Truxal who was the English instructor for my senior year in high school at St. Mary's Seminary Junior College in St. Mary's City, MD. She encouraged me to write poetry and prose, made me an editor on the junior college paper, and, along the way, convinced me to give up my plans to become an electronic engineer and change my college major to journalism instead. Ms. Truxal predicted that after a couple of years as a newspaper reporter I would write books, and while I might make more money as an engineer I would live to regret that choice. I followed her advice but wound up working as a print journalist for more than 60 years before retiring, and finally producing those books. I have no regrets. I hope she would be proud.

Preface

Small towns are special places.

I've lived in my share of them – places like Leonardtown and LaPlata, Maryland and a small village outside Naha, Okinawa.

Such places are small enough to enable residents to develop a sense of community and camaraderie which was absent in the big cities where I lived.

Tybee Island, a small town situated beside the sea – or at the edge of the earth as some like to say – is extra special.

Its residents have created a community of folks who not only welcome, but actually care about one another. Islanders represent a potpourri of people with dramatically different beliefs and backgrounds who congregate comfortably under one enormous, open-minded beach umbrella.

Where else can you find annual events like a Beach Bum Parade (the longest rolling water fight in the world!), a Juneteenth celebration, a Martin Luther King Jr. Parade, an ocean Polar Bear Plunge, and a Pirates' Festival, in addition to active music, dance, art, theatrical and civic groups along with an abundance of wildlife, a pristine beach, and ocean and river recreation?

It's the people, of course, that make Tybee so special. I want to give a special thanks to those who read the first volume in this series, and hence are familiar with my own discovery of the island. A reprint of that introduction is provided below for new readers.

I was in my early 20s when Tybee seduced me.

Situated just down the road from Savannah, more than a few things about the island turned my head.

Her beauty was ubiquitous, from her willowy, windswept dunes to her miles of pristine beach bordering, depending on her mood, either crashing or calmly serene surf, it was a photographer's paradise.

It was paradise in other ways as well for an energetic young reporter for the Savannah Morning News.

Populated by eccentric, hard-drinking party-lovers, its raucous bars made Tybee the polar opposite of what was then Savannah's sleepy ambience.

Preachers and politicians, scions of society and scallywags, lawyers, gamblers, fishermen, musicians, and artists rubbed shoulders on its beaches and in its bistros.

I fell in love with the island, deeply and permanently.

The job at the Savannah newspaper was my first since leaving Tokyo, where from 1957 to 1960 I had pursued post graduate studies in philosophy while working for Pacific Stars & Stripes, the Associated Press and the Okinawa Morning Star.

My shift at the newspaper, covering city hall before being named editor of Savannah Magazine, was from 3 p.m. to 11 p.m. or so, depending on the events of the day.

When my workday ended, there was little happening in Savannah, where only one bar, the Port Royal, was then operating on River Street.

In contrast, Tybee's bars were alive and filled with music-loving, beer-guzzling locals who were quick to befriend anyone on an adjacent bar stool at face value, rarely asking where they were from or what they did for a living.

After hoisting a few, the natives often regaled you with tales of Tybee's past, some of which had an ominous edge.

Semi-inebriated islanders said there had been no rapes or murders on Tybee for years because most miscreants knew how locals dealt with such felonies.

Their stories described how they'd drag malevolent offenders aboard a shrimp boat and drop them off the stern when the shrimpers lowered their nets while heading out to sea.

For lesser offenses like robberies or break-ins, culprits might be hauled over to Little Tybee, buried up to their chests in the sand, have honey poured on their heads, and be left to try to extricate themselves before ants and gulls had a picnic.

I never knew whether the tales were true or simply cautionary warnings, but, like others who heard them, I was not inclined to find out.

With no mandated closing time, Tybee's beach-side bacchanal often lasted till dawn, providing stress relief and a plethora of new pleasures enlivening my existence and expanding my horizons.

More often than many mature folks might find reasonable, I found myself driving back to Savannah with eyes watering from the burning sunrise reflected in the rear-view mirror.

Those were the "good old days" I found on Tybee 62 years ago, before heading north to continue my newspaper career with the Norfolk Virginian-Pilot from 1962 to 1967 and the Washington Post from 1967 to 1992.

Based on that early exposure to Tybee, when it came time to retire from the Post, I headed back to the island, looking for the good vibes I remembered to help me decide what I wanted to do with the rest of my life and where I wanted to do it.

My plan was to hunker down near the beach for a month to get my head around such stuff. That was 30 years ago, and I never left.

Once I realized I was here to stay, I expanded my interests well beyond those initial bar-hopping days. I joined the "Y" and helped start a senior's club there; joined four friends in initiating the annual New Year's Day Polar Bear Plunge which now draws thousands; promoted the first official and now annual New Year's Eve celebration on the South End; helped salvage the old Post Theater when it was about to be demolished; and helped create a DeSoto Beach Hotel exhibit in the Lighthouse Museum to preserve memories of the island's storied old Mediterranean-style hotel.

Along the way I met dozens of islanders who had lived and were still living extraordinary lives and became convinced that their stories should be shared before they were lost forever.

Bitten once again by the writing bug, I started a weekly column in what was then the Savannah newspaper's "Closeup" section called "J.R.'s Island View." The column introduced readers to often little-known but fascinating folks who lived on or near Tybee Island.

Early (circa 1997) fan Mary Slater enjoys Closeup column with morning smoke and coffee.

The columns not only described their impressive accomplishments but told of their escapades and foibles. Based on the positive feedback from readers, the column succeeded in providing its audience with a bit of informative and refreshing reading over morning coffee. Since becoming somewhat more reflective as I've grown considerably longer in the tooth, it occurred to me that those stories, collectively, captured a snapshot of what Tybee was like a quarter century ago.

Many long-time Tybee residents now believe those were the "real" good old days.

This book is a compilation of some those old columns and photos.

They've been assembled in the hope that they may help those who were here at the time savor some pleasant memories and may provide newcomers with a slice of easy-to-swallow island history.

For recent island arrivals, I suspect today will become their own good old days when they think about them 25 years from now, years that will pass far faster than most can imagine.

With luck, the current crop of writers will help them enjoy these treasured memories one day, just as I'm hoping to do with this book.

POSTSCRIPT: You will see postscripts after most chapters to let you know what has happened to the

folks I've written about since I first put their stories to paper.

Some have passed away or moved away, and some have vanished without a trace (that is, without giving me a chance to put them into my witness protection).

If you have information that I do not, please send it my way to P.O. Box 1503, Tybee Island, GA 31328 or jayrose@juno.com.

J.R. Roseberry sits in front of the iconic Tybee Island Lighthouse.

Table of Contents

Basil Jackson -

Islander Was Heroic Pilot in WWII

Teenager Shot Down After 52 Combat Missions

While he hunkers down on toasty Tybee Island this Christmas, Basil Jackson will remember another one 64 years ago in the freezing cold off the coast of Novia Scotia.

It was on December 21, 1941, that he and dozens of other gallant young members of the Royal Canadian Air Force sailed from Halifax, heading for Britain to join the Allied fight for freedom in World War II.

Basil and his fellow flyboys had just completed flight training in Canada, and, yes, "boys" was the operable word for the group. He had just turned 18.

"The RCAF wouldn't take any new pilots who were older than 25," he says.

While the war was red hot, his most vivid memories are of the cold.

Even the fire raging in Basil's belly to join the Big War cooled temporarily as the little freighter he and his buddies were aboard wallowed through the frigid North Atlantic waves.

"We left Halifax in the coldest winter they ever had," he recalls. "The old banana boat we were on had a freezer but there was no heat at all on that thing. It was two weeks of hell."

The forlorn flyers observed a storm-tossed Christmas day with little to celebrate, since Christmas dinner was the last thing on the minds of those leaning over the ship's rails, their green complexions adding a less than cheery color to the holiday season.

Those who managed to sleep aboard the frigid, frantically bobbing boat were awakened in the middle of the night by the roar of big guns mounted on the escort ships.

"They practiced shooting in the middle of the night, but nobody bothered to tell us about it," he says.

The freighter was part of a huge convoy, but halfway through the crossing it, along with the other slow ships, was left behind by the faster vessels.

"We became sitting ducks, but we were very lucky," he says. "We never saw a torpedo."

Despite his discomfort, Basil fared better than most of his seasick comrades, because he had been on and around boats most of his life.

His father, a member of the British diplomatic corps, moved the family to Boston when Basil was 5, and that's where he fell in love with the sea, racing sailboats and working aboard watercraft on weekends and summer vacations.

Just after finishing high school, he crewed on a British ship sailing from Boston to Bermuda.

It stopped off in New York City, where Basil debarked for a stroll on the return trip, and while walking down Fifth Avenue he spotted a recruitment sign for the Royal Canadian Air Force and instantly decided to volunteer, only to be told that at 17, he was too young.

During the several weeks wait until his eighteenth birthday, Basil returned to Boston to inform his parents of his decision before leaving for Canada to undergo flight training.

He spent the next three months learning to fly single- and twin-engine planes, receiving his commission as a "Pilot Officer," the equivalent of a U.S. second lieutenant, before taking that storm-tossed sail to England, where he learned to fly four-engine bombers.

While training in England, the young pilots were assigned small, single-engine, fully aerobatic bi-planes for six weeks during which they could fly whenever they wanted, anywhere in the country.

"They were fun to fly," recalls Basil, noting that his group spent a lot of time in mock aerial combat, emulating the "dog fights" of World War I.

But the navigational training was somewhat harrowing for him and the other pilots coming over from Canada. Because of the pervasive fear of German spies, "there were no signs on roads or anything," he says.

"They wanted to keep locations secret. In case of an

invasion, they didn't want to give the Germans any clue as to where they were," and this led to some unusual problems for foreign pilots.

"Back in Canada, you could fly a thousand miles and not see anything, but you could fly from one end of England to the other in two hours, and there were towns everywhere."

"It was very hard to know where you were. The best way we found was to fly low along railroad tracks to check the name on the train stations."

Occasionally, members of the group would land on a farm to ask directions.

During the early days of the war Basil says most of the flyers from Canada, Australia, and other areas fared fairly well with English girls, but their social life deteriorated when "large numbers of Americans arrived and took over." "They had more money than anybody else. We used to say they were overpaid, overdressed and oversexed."

His own starting pilot's salary was $325 a month, growing to $450 when he reached the rank of captain.

Initially, Basil flew missions in twin-engine Wellington light bombers.

"That was a beautiful plane, but it was slow and had canvas covered wings and no protection, but that's all they had at first," he says.

Later, the teenaged pilot headed a seven-man crew flying four-engine British Lancaster bombers on night raids over France and Germany.

Large groups with up to 1,000 planes flew at an altitude of under 20,000 feet, with no fighter escorts on the missions, and casualties were exceptionally high, especially during the early stages of the war.

"People are used to seeing planes flying in perfect formation in movies, but we didn't do that," he says. "We had a bunch of planes taking off at night flying in the same direction, all of them zig- zagging to take evasive action."

"We'd lost as many as a hundred planes on each mission. I'd venture to say we lost as many planes running into one another as we did from German fighters and flak."

Lost planes were quickly replaced by an intensive British building program turning out 400 bombers a week, but the massive loss of pilots resulted in a severe shortage early on.

"We were more or less cannon fodder," says Basil.

The military's answer to the pilot shortage was to eliminate co- pilots from British planes.

"Since they couldn't afford to lose two pilots at once, they just took the co-pilot's seat out," he says. "I taught my navigator to fly a little in case I was injured, but I never got around to showing him how to land."

The heavy personnel losses took a toll on personal relationships as well. Basil says except for their tight-knit crews, he and other fliers formed few close friendships "because, you know, with the heavy losses, getting too close to someone might affect your flying."

One of the most dangerous assignments on the night raids was handled by the 405th Squadron, known as the Pathfinder Force. Pilots in this squadron flew ahead of the main group of bombers to locate and mark targets by dropping flares.

Basil volunteered to join the Pathfinders.

He flew 52 combat missions, remaining on duty throughout his service although he could have taken home leave after 30 missions.

"That's just what I wanted to do," he says. "I don't know whether I was just young and crazy or gung-ho, but I never thought I would get hurt."

"Every night when you started to fly, until you took off and had your wheels locked up, it was hard on you. You'd be sweaty and all, but as soon as you got airborne, it all disappeared. It was like, 'hey, we're going to have a good run tonight, don't worry about it.' We never had any fear whatsoever after takeoff."

Basil Jackson with model of bomber he piloted on combat missions in World War II.

It appeared that luck was running with the young pilot. While his bomber was frequently hit by flak, only two of those aboard were ever injured.

Basil was one of them.

He was hit in the face by a 50 MM shell, "but it wasn't a big deal," he says. "It bounced off my forehead. I bled a lot, and blood got in my eyes. They took me in for treatment, gave me a Distinguished Flying Cross, and I was back flying in a week."

His bombardier was wounded when "a tracer sliced through his right cheek (as in posterior)," Basil grins, indicating the injury was more embarrassing than serious.

But luck ran out for most of the seven-man crew on the night of February 24, 1944.

They had just completed two bomb runs over Schweinfurt, Germany, and were settling in for the 450-mile flight home when a German fighter plane blew them out of the sky as they crossed the French border.

"It was a ME109 fighter, and he got underneath me pointing up," says Basil. "I flew through his entire stream of bullets. In 10 seconds my aircraft blew up. I had time to yell, 'Get out! Get out!' and that was it."

Four of his crew died in the explosion, which scattered fragments of the plane over the little French village of Bermering.

A large piece of the fuselage landed in the village square as residents scurried for cover. None of the 200 villagers, including 7- year old Pierre Weisse, who watched in awe as debris came crashing down, was injured.

The pilot and two of his crew survived the blast, which blew Basil through the roof of his cockpit, stripping off his shoes and socks in the process.

"You do some dumb things at times like that," he recalls. "You don't know what you're doing. My feet were colder than hell, and I was rubbing them together trying to get them warm. Then I reached for the rip cord on my chest parachute and said, 'Uh Oh...no parachute!"

Basil says he fell 19,000 feet while considering the prospect of plummeting to earth with no parachute.

Finally, with the ground rapidly approaching, he remembered they had recently changed the location of chutes from the chest to the back, and the ripcord handle was now down by his side. Basil yanked the handle, popping his chute open just before he hit the ground. Hard!

"I was knocked out cold," he says. "When I came to, I saw lights from the last of the 1,000 planes on the raid disappearing over the horizon."

Still dazed, he wrapped his frozen feet in pieces of parachute, and while trying to decide what to do next, he heard the clanking sound of a train nearby and hobbled toward it.

Basil figured luck was with him when the train stopped just as he approached, and he spotted an open door on one of the railcars. Struggling in, he managed to slide the door shut, then wrapped himself in the parachute and collapsed, completely exhausted.

Just after he closed the door, the train started up, then slowed to a stop moments later.

While speculating about what was happening and where he was headed, the door was suddenly snatched open by German soldiers who reached in and yanked him out.

Basil smiles somewhat sheepishly as he reveals how the German spotted him so quickly.

"I saw that my parachute was hanging outside the car door when they opened it. It was just blowing around out there for everyone to see."

The Germans hauled him to a nearby interrogation center where he was questioned repeatedly for a week.

"They wanted to know about our missions, staffing, base locations, what I was flying, and information like that," he says. "All I would tell them is my name and that I was a member of the Royal Canadian Air Force."

He was then placed in a cell where his captors alternated pumping in cold and hot air before resuming the interrogation. The process was repeated time and again with the same results.

Finally, an American was brought in to handle the questioning.

"When I asked him what he was doing there he said he just decided to come back to his parents' home when the war started," says Basil. "Then he began asking the same questions and getting the same answers."

"After a while he brought out a big book with my name in it. It had my entire background, with the training I had, my squadron, with whom I flew, where I went on leave, and my whole history."

"I said well, you don't need me anymore, and he said, 'Right, you're on your way,' and sent me off to the prison camp."

The next thing Basil knew he was in Stalag Luft 3, a prisoner-of-war camp just outside Sagan, Germany, which housed captured Allied airmen.

Remember the movie *The Great Escape*? The one in which prisoners dug a tunnel and Steve McQueen jumped a motorcycle over a barbed wire prison fence? Well, this was the same Stalag Luft 3.

There were about 2,000 prisoners in the camp, all housed in barracks containing ten rooms each, with a dozen occupants in every room. Another 8,000 prisoners occupied three adjacent compounds.

Basil helped dig the tunnel depicted in *The Great Escape* and years later, he was invited to Atlanta along with other former POWs for a special viewing of the movie.

It was "pretty good," he says, except for Steve McQueen's "ridiculous" motorcycle jump. "Of course, he was a star and he had to do something."

Prisoners ran their camp "pretty much like a city, under a British group captain who was like a mayor," recalls Basil. "Nobody liked him much. He was cold. One of those stiff-necked types, very proper, and he seemed to always have better food and better clothes than anyone else."

Because of concern that German spies might try to infiltrate their group, the POWs banned new arrivals from talking to anyone until ten other prisoners could verify their identity.

Two spies, neither of whose identity could be verified by prisoners, were discovered while Basil was there.

"They were tried by a court made up of prisoners, found guilty and sentenced to death," he recalls. "It sounds hard, but we were at war, they were spies, and that's what you do with them."

After the spies were disposed of, he and his fellow prisoners were astounded when they were not punished. German officials never referred to the incident, and no further attempt was ever made to infiltrate the camp.

What infuriated the Germans was the mass escape through the tunnel, after which prison officials wreaked their own brand of vengeance on the escapees and those who assisted them.

What had earlier been reasonable treatment and acceptable meals quickly turned to harsh handling and reduced rations of bad food. Basil lost 25 pounds during his 14-month incarceration.

Basil's father signed up with the Canadian Army as a commissioned officer while his son was in prison. Ironically, he served the last year of the war guarding German POWs.

The tunnel Basil helped dig stretched 330 feet, to a

point just beyond the barbed wire fence surrounding the camp, "but we came up a little short," he says. "Our engineers miscalculated. It should have been about 20 feet longer."

The tunnel opened in view of guards patrolling the area, and only two or three could crawl out at a time, just after guards passed by.

The escape tunnel, dubbed "George," started beneath a theater building in the compound. It was one of three under construction at the time.

The one depicted in the movie, which started under a wood stove inside a barracks, was called "Harry," and was actually discovered by the Germans before it was completed.

"I think we intentionally let them find it while we continued to work on the one we really wanted to use," says Basil, who worked on the tunnel beneath the theater six hours a day, along with 19 other prisoners.

Amateur thespians among the prisoners staged plays once a month in the theater, and "they were not bad," he says. "After the war some of the guys who put on the plays started their own theater in London and did rather well."

The diggers devised an ingenious way to dispose of the large volume of dirt removed from their tunnel. They tied the legs of their pajamas at the ankles with slip knots, then filled the legs with dirt. A string was run from the knots up through holes in their pockets, and dirt was released by pulling on the strings as they walked around the exercise yard.

"You had to be careful to match the dirt outside with that from the tunnel, and five or six people always walked behind to shuffle the dirt around," he says.

Basil says the real purpose of the escape was to pull German soldiers from the fight against the Allies by occupying them in a search for escapees.

The original plan called for 250 prisoners to make the escape, which would have tied up a thousand or so German searchers.

Although he labored long and hard on the tunnel project, Basil was not allowed to participate in the escape because rules mandated that prisoners had to be there for at least two years before being eligible for any escape attempt.

That rule may have saved his life.

Problems arose when the Allies dropped bombs on a nearby town, cutting off electricity, and a number of those trying to escape got claustrophobia in the darkness, jamming the tunnel.

Only 85 prisoners got out, and only two of those made it back to England.

Thirty-three escapees were captured, beaten, and hauled back to the prison where they were placed in solitary confinement. The remaining 50 were murdered.

"They were rounded up and taken out in a field where the Germans mowed them down," says Basil. "There was no Geneva Convention or anything like that. They shot those people in cold blood. After the war, all Germans involved in the massacre were identified, tried, and executed."

No further efforts were made to tunnel out of the prison, and conditions remained miserable until Feb. 11, 1945. That's when the prisoners were awakened before daylight and told by prison officials that they could either stay there or march off with an escort of German guards.

After learning that Russian troops were approaching the camp, Basil says virtually all decided to leave with the guards, "most of whom were old and in worse shape than we were. They could hardly keep up with us. I even had to carry the rifle for one of them."

"That was the coldest February of all time. We were freezing and dragging ourselves through the snow, pulling our stuff along with sleds we made out of bed boards and string."

"We marched in that snow for three days. Then it thawed, and we couldn't pull the sleds anymore. We took what we could carry and abandoned them. There were 200 sleds spread all over the place."

"We started out again, sleeping at night in barns or in open fields, until we got to a little town where they crammed us into railroad cars. There were about 100 of us in each car. It was so crowded we had to stand up."

Four days into the trip the train stopped and prisoners were asked if they needed water. Having had none since boarding, all said they did. They got water, but it was taken from the train's engine.

"We were on that train two weeks, and everyone had dysentery," says Basil. "We used one corner of the car, but you can...well, you can just imagine."

The prisoners disembarked in Hamburg, one of the German cities almost totally destroyed in round the clock bombing by Americans during the day and other Allied planes at night.

When Hamburg residents spoke to prisoners passing through their city, the POWs claimed to be fighter pilots, deciding it would be wise not to be connected with the bombing.

The bedraggled band stumbled on for 50 miles before coming to a hill. While resting there they heard the rumble of British tanks and ran to hail them down.

"They gave us food and wine, and three days later hauled us in lorries to the nearest airport where they loaded us aboard planes," says Basil. "We were flying over Paris and into London on VE Day. It was quite something."

After arriving in London, the group spent several weeks undergoing treatment for various medical problems and being fed five meals a day.

Once outfitted with new uniforms and released, Basil and 400 Canadians were instructed to board a ship in South Hampton for the trip back home.

The upper decks of the old freighter were filled with Americans, none of whom had seen any action, while Basil's group was led down deck after deck until they reached the lowest, dankest area of the ship.

At this point the group rebelled, marching back up through the ship and down the gangplank, despite threats from officers trying to keep them on board.

"We told them after what we'd been through, we weren't going to be treated like that," says Basil. "They asked if we understood we could be cashiered out of the service for this and we said, 'Who cares?' They backed down."

Six weeks later the group was ensconced in relatively palatial cabins aboard the French luxury liner Isle de France.

"We had a lovely trip home," he recalls.

Basil took a brief leave and was about to ship out to join Allied forces in the fight against Japan when the

Basil looks over wall displaying memorabilia from war.

war ended.

After his discharge, he attended the University of North Carolina, and had a successful career in the automotive and aircraft manufacturing business.

He married Ann shortly after meeting her on a blind date in Cleveland, Ohio, where he was attending a training session. They have eight children and recently celebrated their 53rd wedding anniversary.

Over the years, Ann Jackson became a highly successful artist, and opened a popular art gallery in Roswell, GA, which is now operated by their three daughters.

Beginning in the early 1990s, the pair spent a dozen years aboard their sailboat, cruising the Atlantic coast from the Bahamas to Maine.

With the passage of time, Basil says his exploits in the war were relegated to occasional thoughts of the distant past. Then, last year, the memories of those days came flooding back when he made a pilgrimage to the little village in France where parts of his plane plummeted to earth so long ago.

His return to Europe to attend a special ceremony on the Fourth of July was considerably more comfortable than that frigid December voyage in 1941.

On his arrival in Bermering, he was warmly greeted by the village mayor, Pierre Weisse, the same man who witnessed the destruction of Basil's bomber as a small boy.

Mayor Weisse, along with other citizens, decided to erect a monument in memory of the four crew members who gave their lives in the war, and Basil was invited to be the guest of honor for the unveiling.

The stone monument is situated near the spot where the largest fragment of the plane's fuselage came to rest in the square, an area now named "Place du Souvenir" to commemorate the event and honor members of the 405th Pathfinder Squadron.

Canadian government and military officials joined the entire village for the ceremony during which Basil was presented a small, polished piece of metal mounted and framed on a special plaque.

It was a fragment from his Lancaster bomber retrieved 60 years earlier.

The plaque now hangs proudly on a wall in his Tybee home, along with other memorabilia from his years as a heroic teenaged bomber pilot.

POSTSCRIPT: Aug. 28, 2010 was declared Basil Jackson Day on Tybee Island in honor of Basil's heroism in World War II. During ceremonies at the Tybee Veterans Monument on Butler Ave. he was presented the Key to the City by Mayor Jason Buelterman. Basil passed away on Sept. 5, 2013, just nine months after his wife, Anne Marie Jackson died. He was eight days short of his 90th birthday.

Carl Looper -

Quiet Man is World Class Athlete

Joins Circus Then Builds His Own

He's a low-keyed, soft-spoken man who pedals his bike about Tybee Island glancing at lawns and smiling broadly at everyone he passes.

Carl Looper is active in the Tybee Recreation Association, and he and his wife, Kathy, are leaders of the Tybee Beautification Association, promoting attractive landscaping by designating island homes as having the "Yard of the Month."

Both retired simultaneously from their careers as special education teachers in Savannah this year. Kathy taught for 30 years; Carl for 24.

Carl chuckles when he recalls how he and his wife became involved with Tybee's "Yard of the Month" program.

One day they awakened to find the award sign mounted on their front lawn. "We were really surprised," he laughs. "It wasn't until a couple of weeks later that a relative admitted he had put it there as a joke."

But the Loopers got the last laugh. That sign inspired them to work hard improving their yard. Several months later they won the award legitimately and have been active in the association ever since.

Kathy and Carl Looper with their yard of the month sign.

Carl simply seems to be a good neighbor, a pleasant person you'd like to get to know.

But there's more there...much more!

Despite his lethargic demeanor, Carl has led an eye-popping vagabond's life sprinkled with world records and gymnastic derring-do.

And he's still a champion athlete, having recently won several events in Savannah's Golden Olympics for those 55 and older.

While he personifies the friendly, laid-back attitude of a life-long Tybee resident, Carl was born in Monterey, Tennessee, a small town between Knoxville and Nashville.

His parents worked on a tobacco farm until both took jobs with General Motors. They were transported to work each day by a special train to a GM plant in Indiana.

Carl remained with his parents in Tennessee until he was 10, walking six miles round trip each day to grade school, which may have contributed to his physical prowess in later life.

Ultimately the family moved to Anderson, Indiana, near Indianapolis, to be closer to their work.

While in high school, Carl lettered in wrestling and track, running low hurdles, relays and using his heavily muscled legs to launch himself in the long jump.

"My mother used to tell me and my brother that she'd put us up against anyone when it comes to playing," he laughs.

Carl did a lot of playing in those days, especially with yo-yos.

Looper could "Loop the Loop," "Walk the Dog," "Rock the Baby," "Shoot the Moon" and perform virtually all the other tricks known to devotees of the tethered toy.

Once, he won $1,000 in head-to-head competition and that was big money in those days.

He became so adept with the toy that the Duncan Yo-Yo Company hired him as a performer/demonstrator to promote their product.

Carl says he's delighted with the recent rediscovery and growing popularity of yo-yos, so don't be surprised if you find him gearing up for big time competition again.

"I was in a dime store once trying to go for a record 10 "Round the Worlds" (he held the world record at the time with a sequence of nine) and I threw the yo-yo out so hard it broke the string and smashed a light fixture," he grins. "The owner wasn't real happy about that."

Carl also appeared on the Ted Mack Amateur Hour TV show with an acrobatic team as a teenager.

After high school he joined his parents in working on the production line at General Motors for a while before enrolling in Indiana State University in the late 1950s.

Carl was named the school's All-Around Gymnastics Champion and held the world record for a "hand stand high jump." Beginning in a handstand, he cleared a bar almost 18 inches high, then landed again in a hand stand.

Carl seems to enjoy getting in some ping-pong practice.

He was also a YMCA handball champion and was named Indiana State Amateur Ping-Pong Champion in 1960.

Then he dropped out of college to do what most young men only dream about. Carl joined the Clyde Beatty Cole Brothers Circus and toured with the company for three years as an acrobat/clown/trapeze artist.

He drew wild applause from audiences with his one-armed handstand and handstand strolls down a long flight of stairs. He also performed tumbling and adagio acts and served as "catcher" for trapeze performers when he wasn't cavorting as a clown.

The circus wintered near his home, and Carl hung out with performers and riggers as a kid, always yearning to join up.

But he found travelling around the country with the circus wasn't the exciting, carefree life he had fantasized about.

"It was tough," he says. "I enjoyed performing, but it was a hard life. We had 12-hour days with everyone working to set up the circus in the morning, then performing at night and taking it down and moving on to the next town."

Carl steps out on stilts as Uncle Sam.

What he learned in those days has stuck with him, however. Carl is a member of the Savannah Shrine's Alee Temple and continues to perform as a clown for special events. He can also be easily spotted at virtually every parade or festival on Tybee meandering about on tall stilts dressed as Uncle Sam.

Carl spent years building a 40-foot scale model circus layout with 20,000 parts, including a thousand miniature animals, 3,000 people and "big tops" on which the canvas can be raised.

Many of his molded animals and people were acquired from Belgium and are now quite valuable since the molds no longer exist.

Carl's miniature circus drew enthusiastic crowds when he erected it several years ago in Savannah's Civic Center during a promotion for the Ringling Bros. Circus.

He was also scheduled to erect the layout at Oglethorpe Mall but canceled when officials refused to permit him to stay with his model overnight.

"I don't like to leave it unattended," he says. "Somebody's always stealing something and some of the antique pieces can't be replaced."

Departing from the norm, Carl ran away from the circus to join the Army.

His gymnastics exploits followed him, however, and organizers of USO shows frequently enlisted his services to entertain the troops.

"They even pulled me out of the field during boot camp maneuvers," he laughs, noting that his commanding officer was somewhat less than ecstatic when this occurred.

Following his discharge, Carl returned home to obtain his bachelor's degree at Anderson College in Anderson, Indiana, where he was a star on the school's gymnastics team, then earned his master's degree in physical education from Ball State University.

He was a serious weightlifter during those days, winning two national collegiate titles in power lifting. Carl bench pressed 395 pounds, while hoisting 535 pounds in the squat position, and 650 pounds in the dead lift.

He weighed 181 pounds and in 1969 was ranked among the top 10 power lifters in the world.

There were also a few less serious moments during Carl's weightlifting days.

"My friends and I used to amuse ourselves picking up VWs and putting them on the sidewalk," he laughs. "With those round bumpers they had wonderful grips and were real easy to lift."

Later, he was appointed to the weightlifting organizing committee for the 1984 Olympics in Los Angeles.

After graduation, he taught physical education in Hamilton, Ohio grade schools, while serving as head trainer for the Hamilton Mini Circus for Children and a caller for square dances on the side.

His summers were spent in Sarasota, Florida, where he studied and filmed circus acts in order to incorporate them in the children's circus.

"We had children doing trapeze, unicycle, and tumbling acts," he recalls, noting that while he was in Ohio tumbling and gymnastics were part of the school curriculum.

His students became so proficient that they appeared on national television five times and often put on half-time shows for professional basketball games.

One 16-year-old student worked constantly with Carl in his back yard learning to ride taller and taller unicycles.

When the one-wheeled cycle reached impressive heights, Carl climbed atop the seat where, he says, "you could see all over the city!"

His student ultimately made history and was written up in the Guinness Book of World Records when he rode a 34-foot, 10-inch unicycle for 20 feet.

Carl was touring bistros in Underground Atlanta on a break from his Ohio activities in 1975 when he struck up a conversation with a lady he enticed to the dance floor. She turned out to be the personnel director of Chatham-Savannah Schools and asked if he would be interested in teaching here.

"I said I'd think about it, and when I returned home, a contract was in the mail," he says.

Familiar with and fond of the area since his Army days when he joined busloads of troops from Fort Gordon for trips to Tybee, Carl jumped at the chance. And Carl jumps pretty good.

He moved to the beach and commuted to his initial job as a physical education teacher at Romana Riley Elementary School in the old VW van he drove here from Ohio.

Carl met Kathy during a lunch break at Jacob G. Smith Elementary School where she taught visually impaired students. Carl, who routinely moved from school to school, frequently ate there.

"We were in the lunchroom, and I just saw her and asked her to go with me to see *Alabama* at the Civic Center," he recalls. "She accepted, and the rest is history!"

Shortly after taking the Romana Riley job, he learned there was a special education center for handicapped children just down the street, which was anxious to start a modified physical education program.

The peripatetic gymnast again leaped at the opportunity and wound up teaching handicapped children at the Exceptional Child Center for the next 22 years.

Kathy, who continued teaching the visually impaired for even longer, is a life-long area resident.

Her parents married in 1933 while her father was stationed at Fort Screven where he was in charge of turning the lighthouse light on each night.

Kathy and Carl reside in a house built on the foundation of the old Fort Screven Chapel, just a block or so from her father's old residence.

They believe their extended careers working with special students turned out to be the most rewarding experience of their lives and proved especially beneficial for area children.

Carl modified his regular teaching techniques to enable students to play wheelchair basketball and soccer.

Blind students played a special version of T-Ball where the ball and the bases contained beepers to guide them.

Matches between his students and the local minor league teams and even the Atlanta Braves were staged occasionally, with the professional players wearing blindfolds.

"The kids really enjoyed that," says Kathy.

Carl checks application papers for Special Olympics.

Carl organized the Special Olympics in 1976 for mentally challenged children in Savannah, starting with 30 children competing in Daffin Park. With Carl serving as the local and later area coordinator for 14 years, the event now draws about 500 participants, and a number of his Special Olympians have become winners in the International Summer Special Olympics Games.

He also founded the Special Games for physically handicapped youngsters in the early 1990s.

Those events featured wheelchair races and ball and Frisbee throws and remained popular for several years until funding ran out.

He says one of his fondest sports memories involves his team's participation in the State Special Olympics at Warner Robins.

"One of the girls in the 100-yard dash stopped in the middle of the race for some reason and the rest of the competitors stopped and waited there for her to catch up," he smiles, noting that the girl went on to win the race.

"They don't care what color ribbon they win," he says. "They just enjoy participating."

"One of the things they enjoy most is the hugs they receive at the end of each event," adds Kathy. "We call the volunteers 'Official Huggers' and they enjoy it as much as the kids when they hug them and walk them over to their medals."

During the trip back to Savannah Carl divided up the funds left over from their trip among the 35 participants and stopped at a grocery store.

"You know what?" he asks. "You'd expect them to load up their carts with candy and stuff, wouldn't you? They didn't! They loaded up with mostly fruit. They just loved fruit."

But teaching and directing athletic events were not the only things Carl did for area children.

He frequently donned different outfits on holidays to entertain them, wearing a gorilla costume on Halloween and a Santa Claus suit for Christmas.

"That went real well for a long time until one year when one of my students looked down and saw I was wearing my tennis shoes," laughs Carl. "When he spotted them, he yelled out, 'That's not Santa Claus! That's Mr. Looper. He's got his Converse All Stars on. From then on, I had to wear black leather shoes."

Both Carl and Kathy retired from teaching simultaneously at the close of school this year. Hundreds came to honor them at their retirement party in Savannah's Alee Temple.

Despite retirement, an old shoulder injury, and a circuitous and long road traveled, Carl has not abandoned his interest in either exercise or athletic competition.

He disdains the use of an automobile on Tybee, travelling by jogging or on a bicycle instead, and keeps in shape by helping to maintain the large pool complex at the Lighthouse Landings condominiums.

Carl's continuing competitive streak was on display this year in Savannah's "Golden Olympics" for those 55 and older.

Carl concentrates on work at condo complex pool.

At 58, it was his first appearance in the competition, and he won the softball and Frisbee throws and the basketball shoot.

He also came in second in an event he can't recall. Apparently coming in second seems like losing when you've always been a winner.

This September Carl will participate in the state games at Warner Robins, which features golf, tennis, and ping-pong among other competitive events.

"I'm planning on taking up golf again after a long time, and I'm definitely going to compete in ping-pong," he says enthusiastically. "I used to be pretty good at that."

If he wins there, he'll go on to Disney World for the nationals in December.

And Carl continues to work on his miniature circus, building and repairing model tents and horse drawn wagons for the layout which is mounted on four-by-eight sheets of plywood.

He's also developed an interest in yet another sport in which his eyes scan the skies while a bunch of his friends do the racing.

The sport involves raising and racing homing pigeons.

His birds compete in September and March, with those born this year racing in the former month and older ones in the latter. The prize birds are loaded up and ferried as far as 600 miles away for competitions in which they are released by a "liberator" and carefully logged in on special clocks when they arrive back at

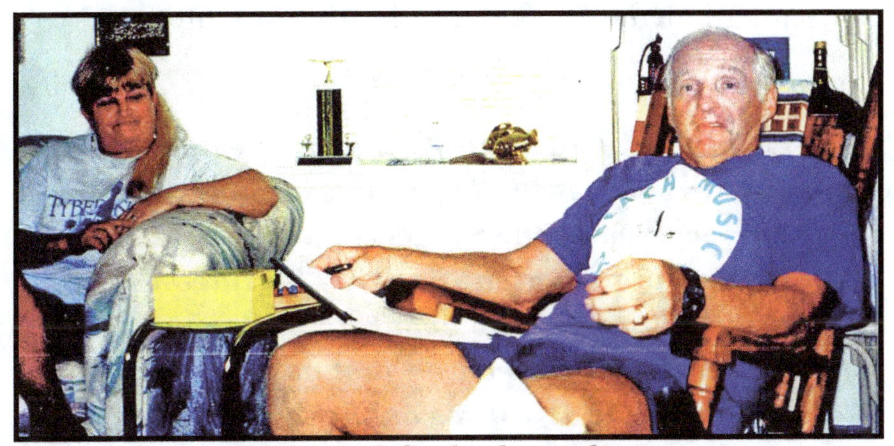

Kathy and Carl relax at home.

their nests.

Carl's penchant for pigeons was sparked by happenstance during the 1984 Los Angeles Olympics.

"They gave me three pairs of pigeons which were among the thousands released at the opening ceremonies, and that got me started," he says.

While Carl says he is the only person involved in the sport on Tybee, there are three clubs in the Savannah area and numerous enthusiasts all over the country.

"It's a good sport," he says. "It sure keeps you at home!"

And that's where Carl and Kathy intend to remain, maintaining their attractive yard and prompting others to do the same while Carl tends his pools, pigeons, and circus when he's not biking about cultivating friends and yards.

Only his lingering lust for competition in those Golden Olympics can lure him away now, and even if he falters in the September games, this nice, quiet man already has enough medals and memories to last a lifetime.

POSTSCRIPT: Carl and Kathy Looper organized a special Tybee Senior Olympics several years after this was written. Staged in Jaycee Park, with the golfing segment held at the Bacon Park course in Savannah, the event drew dozens of the island's seniors who seemed just as delighted with their ribbons and trophies as those youngsters were at the earlier competition in Atlanta. Meanwhile, the Loopers continue to keep their yard in award-winning shape.

Olivera Lee -

Shuuu! Let's Keep This a Secret

Olivera Lee

Nonagenarian
Islander
Still Active

It may sound like an oxymoron, but don't be deceived. Olivera Lee is a very young 91, although she doesn't want you to discuss her age.

This energetic, self-effacing lady could very easily pass for 60 or so, and she would just as soon folks thought of her that way.

It's not because she's vain, as might be the case with many of us who would prefer to appear younger than our years.

Olivera doesn't have a vain bone in her slender body. She is, if anything, far too modest.

She's even somewhat embarrassed about being interviewed, claiming she's done nothing special and can't imagine why anyone would be interested in hearing about her.

The problem is that when people learn her age, "They look at me and suddenly see the wrinkles and they want me to stop doing things," she frowns. "They think I'm too old for this or that."

She mowed the ample lawn at her home on Tybee up until last year when neighbors discovered her age and insisted that she stop doing it because they feared she might hurt herself.

"I really enjoyed that, but now I have somebody do it for me because I don't want to worry people," Olivera says.

But she still does her own gardening on sunny days, takes long walks about the island, "and I do my own housework and do my own hair."

Olivera enjoys going to the Tuesday Night Supper Club at Fort Screven, and is an active member of the Tybee Historical Society, Tybee Optimist Club, Trinity Chapel United Methodist Church, and the Candler Hospital Auxiliary.

She was also an enthusiastic participant in the Tybee Square Dance Club until it was disbanded because the regular caller moved away and membership fell off.

Olivera is now supporting a movement to reactivate the club and plans to be out there again if the effort is successful.

"It's really a good exercise," she says.

This nifty nonagenarian doesn't plan to tell anyone else how old she is, lest they try to interfere with some of her pleasurable activities, so make sure you don't either! Let's make this our and Olivera's little secret.

Heck, if word of her age got out, somebody might even try to stop her from driving.

Olivera drives into Savannah at least once a week to perform volunteer work at Candler Hospital, among other things.

"I drive as well now as I did when I was 50 years old," she insists.

They might even try to discourage her from participating in the Olympics, for gosh sakes! That would be a pity since a lot of Islanders are looking forward to her taking part in the upcoming Tybee Golden Olympics. Most are even willing to lay odds that she'll win whatever competition she's involved in.

One event she's planning to enter now is the one-mile walk, which she has been training for, inadvertently, since moving to Tybee in the early 1980s.

Olivera started walking for fun and exercise immediately after her arrival. She used to stroll several miles a day, but is down to about a mile now, having been slowed just a trifle by her recent encounter with an ornery little circulatory problem in her right foot.

But a mile is enough for these Olympics. She'll be competing in the 90 and above age bracket. It's a pretty safe bet she can bring home the bacon in any contest with those in that age group.

You might want to drop by the Golden Olympics in Jaycee Park on April 10.

"Champion Olympian Olivera" has a nice ring to it.

Olivera was “born and raised in Statesboro and that was like living in the country then,” she says. “Statesboro was not developed like it is now.”

She was born on December 14, 1908 (“I’m a Sagittarius,” she smiles) in a house on Denmark Street, and named for her grandmother. But she hasn’t been back for some time and wonders if the old house is still there.

“I’m told that the street still exists,” she says. “I lived in Statesboro ‘til I was 14 and my father moved to Savannah where I spent the rest of my single life.”

“My father bought a house on Ogeechee Road back when it was in the country. I think it was the second house to be built out there, and we had a good bit of property.”

Her single life didn’t last long, however. Olivera married Randal, a railroad man (the old Seaboard Coast Line), when she turned 17.

“I’m a little embarrassed to admit I got married when I was just 17,” she smiles. “Back then, if you waited until you were 21, you were considered an old maid.”

She says her folks accepted Randal right away.

It didn’t hurt that her father, like Randal, was a career employee with the railroad.

Olivera and her husband moved to his hometown of Waycross soon after they were married.

That was in the midst of the Depression and the newlyweds were soon forced to leave Georgia in search of employment for Randal when the railroad laid him and most of his fellow workers off.

An uncle in Ohio said he could find work in that area so they headed north to weather the bad times.

"He found work with a boiler manufacturer in a little town just outside of Akron, Ohio," she recalls, noting that they returned to Waycross when the economy improved a couple of years later and the railroad started hiring again.

Olivera claims she's been coming to Tybee "for what seems like my entire life."

Just after her father passed away in 1949, her mother purchased a two-story beach cottage on 17th Terrace for $8,000, and Olivera and her family started visiting frequently over the years.

"Any time we wanted to come down we just picked up and came," she says. "We never even asked if it was OK."

"That was a wonderful time down here on the island. Hunter Airfield was activated, and there were a lot of military people down. It wasn't like it is now. There were not a lot of drugs and alcohol, and nobody locked their doors then. Now you don't go to the post office without locking your doors!"

"For entertainment we'd go on the rides and just kind of visit with friends. There weren't many eating places back then, and we just enjoyed each other."

Her mother used to rent space on the porch to soldiers for a dollar a night on weekends, and she made lots of friends, according to Olivera, who says her mother

Olivera Lee sips tea at her island home.

"never had any trouble at all."

Later, Olivera's children, a son and two daughters, spent school vacations with their grandmother at the beach.

"My son, Raleigh, used to work at the hotdog stand at the Pavilion skating rink summers when he was in high school," she recalls, and when her daughter, Mary, attended the University of Georgia, she brought her friends down from college.

Olivera and Randal purchased their own beach house in 1974, and Olivera moved there permanently in 1982, shortly after her husband passed away.

"I haven't had any problems living alone," she says. "A lot of people seem to sit back and grieve and worry about what they can't do now, but I've been busy ever since he passed away. My work as a volunteer gave me an outlet with other people, and I'm just busy with what I'm doing now."

"You can't bring back what you've had, but I'm satisfied doing what I'm doing, and I've always loved Tybee. I never want to leave it. I don't live a very colorful life, but I'm happy with just what I'm doing now."

Once her children were grown and completed their education, including graduate school, Olivera began her own career, starting nurses training when she was 50 years old.

"I'd wanted to do that for many years, but when you were married in my day and you had children, you didn't do that," she says.

She continued her nursing career for almost 13 years before she retired.

While it's hard to imagine, she seems sincere when she claims to have accomplished very little in her life.

When she learned her family was planning a special party at the Tybee Shrine Club for her 90th birthday, she says her biggest concern was that no one would show up!

"I had never had a birthday party because I had never thought about birthdays," she said. "I just knew I had a birthday coming up and that was it. But they had to tell me they were planning a birthday so we could make up a list of people to invite, and that was what I was worried about... what if nobody came? I really did worry about that."

Her fears were clearly misplaced. It was an impressive party with considerably more of her friends - well over 100 - in attendance than the impressive number of candles on her cake.

"That was a special occasion," she smiles. "It was really nice, but I don't need another one because I'm not going to count birthdays."

And if the adulation with which she was showered at that party was not sufficient proof of her success, a letter from her son, Raleigh, leaves no doubt.

The letter, sent to Olivera on Mother's Day in 1996 reads:

"Dear Mama,

"You know, there just aren't any cards out there that would tell you how much I appreciate you as my mother. In fact, there aren't really any words out there that do that either. But, aside from being the best that I can, it's the only way to tell you how much I love you.

"I feel so lucky that I have a mother I not only love, but admire, so much. It would be easy to love you, but you might also be a good-for-nothing low-down slob. I'm always proud to say that my mother is at the top of her class.

"Everybody who knows me knows my mother. They know how pretty you still are, how you take such good care of yourself, how bright your little eyes are, and how good you are to me. I always hope they say, 'so that's why Raleigh is such a good man,' and I bet they do.

"You are my hero and my role model. I want to be like you; in many ways, I already am. But I keep trying to become as good as you have become. I'm so happy that I can see my life before me if I just keep following your example.

"So, quit worrying and never fret over what you think you didn't teach me. It's finally all sinking in, and it was always right. I know my children will benefit from your influence; they already have, I think. If you ever have any doubts about yourself or think you haven't lived up to what you had hoped to achieve, just remember this:

"I want nothing more in my life than to be as good

as you are as a citizen, provider, parent, teacher, and role model. What more can I say?

"I love you, Raleigh.

"Have a wonderful Mother's Day."

Olivera's justifiably proud of her son and his letter, and it would be difficult for most of us to find any greater confirmation of success.

It's OK to talk about that letter, the upcoming Olympics and other stuff involving Olivera, but remember, mum's the word on her age.

POSTSCRIPT: Olivera NeSmith Lee passed away on Oct. 1, 2006, and was buried in Bonaventure Cemetery. She was 98-years-young.

Cullen Chambers -

Keeping the Lighthouse Shining Bright

Expert Shepherds Landmark Preservation

He keeps the light, but he wants it dark. Well, black really. Or almost black, with a small band of white about three quarters of the way up.

That's the way the Tybee Lighthouse looked in 1916.

A lighthouse painting pattern is known as its "day mark" and serves as a daytime navigational aid to passing ships, letting them know where they are at a glance.

Cullen Chambers, a dark and dapper man whose youthful good looks belie his age, is the director of the Tybee Island Historical Society and Tybee Lighthouse. It's his job to oversee one of the best-known historical sites on the East Coast.

Part of his charter is to research its history, plan its preservation and restoration, and supervise that restoration work on the lighthouse and its surrounding complex of buildings.

Spearheading the effort to raise funds for the work is no small part of his assignment. The overall rehabilitation is expected to cost a million dollars.

Cullen, who has held his position for about three years, lives close to his work. He's within the shadow, or the beam, of the light most of the time.

He and his wife, Christine, reside in a lightkeeper's cottage behind the lighthouse gift shop, just a few feet from the base of the lighthouse itself. It was originally built in 1885.

Cullen could be called a man of many lights.

He's considered the country's leading authority on

Cullen Chambers discusses lighthouse renovation.

lighthouses and their restoration.

“I don’t know of any individual who’s worked on more lighthouses than I have,” he says. “I didn’t intend for it to be that way. It just happened.”

Cullen started his lighthouse restoration efforts in Key West, Florida and worked his way north, lingering in the historic town of St. Augustine, Florida before landing on Tybee.

Along the way, he supervised work on the restoration of other historic buildings and artifacts from the sea.

But the Tybee project has a special place in his heart. For one thing, it includes part of an old fort, and “my real love is coastal fortifications,” he says.

Tybee’s lighthouse and its associated support complex are already quite unusual, and restoring the 1916 paint design will make it the only lighthouse in the country exhibiting that day mark.

And it’s one of only a handful of lighthouses still serving as navigational aids and tourist attractions. Of the original 15 in Georgia, there’s only one other, located on St. Simons Island.

“Tybee’s is one of only 20 intact light stations in America,” says Cullen.

Support buildings at other light stations were torn down in the 1960s and 70s because the Coast Guard lacked funds to maintain them, but it continued to operate the Tybee light station until 1987, maintaining all the buildings and making it possible to initiate the current restoration.

"It's incredible that its remained," says Cullen, noting that "this site, along with about a dozen others, has been nominated for National Historic Landmark status, the highest designation you can get for a historic site. We're already on the National Register."

Perhaps the most important contributors to his affinity for Tybee, however, are the island's residents.

"I have never seen an organization that has benefited more from volunteerism than this one has," he says. "I've never seen a more consistently dedicated group of volunteers. They'll come out in the heat of summer and the dead of winter to work at the lighthouse and museum, and we couldn't even consider the restoration project without them."

Initial rehabilitation work begins the last week in January when the old paint - there have been 11 coats covering the bricks inside the lighthouse over the years - is removed and the mortar between the bricks repointed for the first time in 130 years.

Half of the estimated $350,000 cost of lighthouse refurbishment, which will include repainting and repairs to the interior circular steel staircase leading to the light on top, has already been raised.

Cullen says he has set a personal priority of raising funds for the remaining work by year's end. That's a major mandate.

"To give you an example," he says, "Florida had a preservation budget of $11 million a year state-wide. Georgia's preservation budget is $280,000. This project will cost $1 million and you can see how long it would

Work underway on re-painting Lighthouse.

take if the funds were raised from a state level."

Cullen said he's grateful to Georgia State Rep. Burke Day, who lives on Tybee, for getting a $15,000 grant from the legislature for the light station last year. The historical society raised funds to match that allocation.

"I hope he'll go back this year and get more funding to shorten the process of my going around begging for funds," says Cullen. "This project needs to be attended to.

"What I have to do is marry federal, state, corporate, private and individual donations to give us the support we need, first to restore the lighthouse and then, ultimately, the whole site."

There is a real sense of urgency to his fund-raising efforts.

"We can't afford to continue at the pace we're going, shutting down the operation each year to do part of the work, then reopening again, and expect to generate the interest and visitation we need to continue the operation of this light station," Cullen warns. "It's not cost effective to do it this way, and the longer we wait the more damage it (the lighthouse complex) gets."

Since it must be closed during the paint removal and stair repairs, with the height of the tourist season approaching, there's considerable pressure to expedite the process.

Those tourist dollars - an estimated gross of $240,000 is generated annually from the sale of books and gift shop items and fees for admission to the lighthouse and museum - are needed to maintain the facility, and any money left over after operational expenses is set aside for restoration.

Once the project is completed, Cullen expects visitation to increase from the current 70,000 a year to 100,000 or so.

Cullen, dressed in original lighthouse keepers uniform, discusses renovation project.

The historical society took control of the site in 1987 and increased visitation from a few hundred that year to 20,000 in 1989. The number is now held to about 70,000 by limiting hours of operation to minimize wear and damage to the facility.

Cullen spent more than a year determining the condition of the complex, creating a master plan describing its needs and the proper sequence of work and researching historical information to be used as a guideline for architects.

It was only after completing the research that he was able to formulate a comprehensive rehabilitation plan

Cullen climbs Lighthouse stairs on inspection tour.

and determine the funding required.

Now it's time to get on with the work.

But, despite the pressure to complete the job, work on a structure of such historical significance can't be rushed since its structural integrity must be maintained.

"You'd never just go in and sandblast it," says Cullen, who cringes at the thought.

He's made an extensive study of paint removal processes, interviewed half a dozen contractors, and conducted tests of their removal techniques on patches of brick inside the lighthouse.

Cullen says he is optimistic about one of the final tests conducted in late January by the same company that did recent cleanup work on the Statue of Liberty.

"They use a light caustic agent with a base of bicarbonate of soda," he said, noting that in addition to using the process on the famous New York monument and on old brick, "they've been able to remove graffiti from glass without causing etching."

Until the paint is removed from the interior walls, the

extent of damage caused by years of weathering and water seepage won't be known, but Cullen remains optimistic.

"I've examined it superficially and there's not as widespread damage as I've seen in other lighthouses, but we don't know for sure with it being covered up with so much paint, and we want to be assured that any process we use in removing the old material will not adversely affect the application of the new," he says.

But Cullen is concerned that if the restoration work is not done soon, the structure will become unsafe for visitation by tourists.

Years have worn the stucco on the exterior walls, permitting water to migrate through, and rust occurs when it gets to the metal work in the structure.

"That expanding metal causes the brick around it to start to crumble," he says. "That brings more moisture in, which causes more damage to the metal, which causes more damage to the brick. It perpetuates itself.

"We must do something to save this lighthouse now. It won't fall down, but it would only be a matter of a couple of years before it is unsafe for public access.

"We need the revenue to operate the museum and light station for educational purposes and because it's one of only a few lighthouses that are open to public visitation.

"We want the end result to be a lasting memorial not only to the light keepers who have served here but to the dedicated men and women who have served on the board of directors for so many decades and really scrimped and saved, and the volunteers who came out every day of the week to cut our operational costs so that every cent we can raise is dedicated to the restoration."

Part of the initial restoration will include removal of the porch at the lighthouse entrance, which was built in 1967. This will return the structure to its original design in line with prospective National Landmark status.

Cullen hopes the first phase will be completed and the structure reopened to the public by mid-February.

Many visitors think work on the exterior painting is already underway because of the difference in color on the seaside and land-side facades.

"But the lighter paint you see on the elevation facing the ocean is just where the elements have literally sandblasted the paint off," explains Cullen.

"The wind and rain have blasted that coating down to nearly the surface." The paint pattern on the exterior of the lighthouse has been changed six times since 1867, each time altering its day mark and requiring the Coast Guard to change its navigational charts.

Initially, it was all white. In 1887 the base was painted black. In 1914 the top was painted black, along with the base, with a large white band in between. In 1916 the black was expanded, creating a smaller white band, which is the plan for the current restoration. In 1965, that design was changed to a gray top and white bottom.

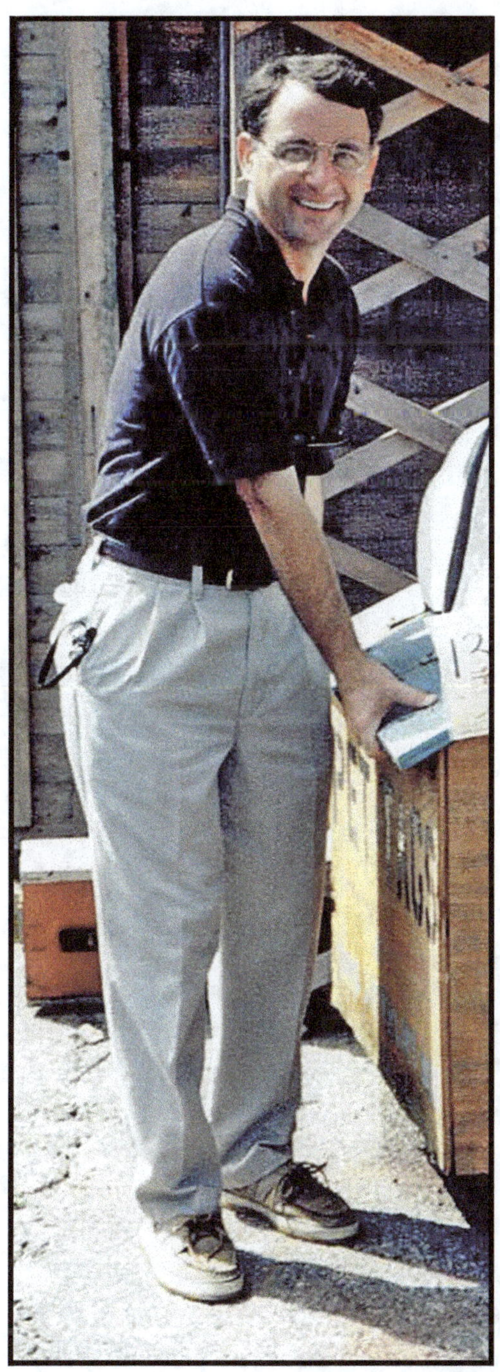

Cullen at work on Lighthouse museum.

The present painting scheme, with a white bottom and black top, was adopted in 1969.

Cullen has been working with the Coast Guard for more than two years to receive permission to return to the 1916 design. He's gotten verbal approval but exterior painting must be delayed until he gets formal, written approval.

Five U.S. lighthouses have the same day mark as Tybee's current one, while returning to the pattern which existed from 1916 to 1965 will make its day mark unique.

Cullen estimates it will cost another $700,000 to restore the 1881 vintage head keepers house, the 1885 first assistant's house, and a smaller second assistant's house which dates back to 1861 when it was used as a Confederate Army barracks.

The "summer kitchen" building, constructed in 1812 and used as a shared kitchen by families of the three lightkeepers on duty simultaneously until 1910, will also be restored, along with a garage and a small fuel storage building.

The fuel building was constructed in 1890 to store kerosene, to which the light was converted in 1887. Prior to that time, mineral spirits or lard were used to operate the light. It was finally converted to electricity in 1933.

The 1,000 watt bulb and its Fresnel lens are still maintained by the Coast Guard. This fixed light gives Tybee its "night signature" identification for ships. Other lighthouses may use rotating, blinking, blinking and rotating, or colored lights for their night signature.

While many similar lenses are now in museums, Tybee's original Fresnel lens, installed in 1867, is still in use. It is one of only 13 still utilized as an active aid to navigation in the United States.

The electric system has proven highly reliable over the years, but it does have a downside, according to Cullen, who says visitors have found the switch which operates it and have occasionally turned it off.

He's taking care of that problem as part of the rehabilitation project. Wiring will be changed "to minimize contemporary intrusions on the lighthouse" and will be so inaccessible that you can pretty much forget about trying to find that switch.

While this is Cullen's third lighthouse project, following Key West and St. Augustine, he has directed restoration of an old high school and served as consultant for a number of projects, including a Civil War fort in Key West. He also served as curator of another historic Key West fort.

And he has served as an adviser on the treatment and preservation of metal artifacts retrieved from a Spanish galleon off the coast of Florida and restoration of a cemetery and a church in St. Augustine.

Currently, Cullen is consulting on restoration of a lighthouse on Sapelo Island and the Currituck light on the coast of North Carolina. Careful to avoid any appearance of conflict of interest, he charges no fee for such consultation.

Cullen takes a break at Tybee Lighthouse.

While it seems Cullen is creeping north occupationally, he claims his wife has put her foot down as far as any permanent migration from Tybee.

Cullen met Christine while working on the Key West project, which he undertook after graduating from Florida State University with a degree in government and history.

He initially did restoration in Key West on a voluntary basis working with Howard England, a self-taught architect whom Cullen describes as "an absolutely incredible individual."

"He was a combat Marine Corps photographer in World War II" and working with him "was probably more of a learning experience for me than any other I've had, including at the university."

Originally from Arkansas, Cullen is one of seven children, including an identical twin brother who works in the computer industry and who Cullen claims "obviously has the brains in the family." The family moved frequently because his father was a naval officer.

"Most folks think I'm from Boston," he says. "That's where I was principally reared."

Christine met him when she visited her sister, who was working with Cullen in Key West.

Later, she again visited her sister, who had moved to St. Augustine, while he was working there, and that's when they really got together and were married in 1995.

"It was destiny," claims Cullen. "She is probably my best friend."

And while he may wander far afield on consulting work, he endorses his wife's commitment to remaining on this island. "We have really grown to love Tybee," he says. "I have never lived in an area where people are

Work on exterior of Lighthouse nears completion.

so community minded. We have a real sense of kinship. This is a wonderful place to live."

It looks like the light keeper and his best friend are here to stay, while working hard to leave the light on for us all.

POSTSCRIPT: Cullen oversaw the complete restoration of the Lighthouse and each of the buildings at the Light Station after which the Lighthouse was featured on a U.S. postage stamp. At the time of his death of an apparent heart attack on Jan. 20, 2014, he was spearheading the successful effort to restore the historic Tybee Post Theater.

Dale Williams & Debbie Kearney -

Kayaking Couple Has a Lot in Common

Love & Kayaks Drew Them To the Sea

Dale Williams

Debbie Kearney

With all they have in common, they seemed destined to be together, but 20 years passed before they finally made the connection.

Although Debbie Kearney was born in Florida and Dale Williams in Kentucky, both had parents who were involved with the U.S. Space Program in Huntsville, Alabama, where they grew up.

Debbie's dad specialized in "black box" flight systems for a company doing contract work for the space program, while Dale's dad was employed by NASA.

Both attended college at the University of Alabama, Huntsville, where each majored in psychology.

Both are also enamored of sea kayaking, a sport at which they excel, and they are now literally surrounded by kayaks.

Debbie spends her free time plying area waters in her state-of-the-art kayak made of Kevlar.

Dale spends not only his free time, including vacations involving extended kayak camping trips with Debbie, but also his working hours in and around the tiny watercraft.

He owns and operates Sea Kayak Georgia, one of the largest kayak teaching and camping companies in the country.

It was during their psychology courses at the university, which both attended on academic scholarships, that they first met more than 20 years ago.

They dated at the time and, according to Debbie, were "right at the edge of romance."

Although Alabama's stars sprinkled them, it was just a dusting rather than a full-blown fall.

Each had an agenda, which required their life's partnership to be held in abeyance for two decades.

Debbie went on to obtain her doctorate in psychology from the University of Georgia, while Dale, an indomitable outdoorsman, remained in Alabama, where he established a horse ranch.

Sticking with her chosen profession, Debbie ultimately wound up in Savannah, where she worked for the state before entering private practice.

She is now affiliated with the Savannah Psychotherapy Center.

Dale, whose attention span was somewhat more limited, gave up his horses after a couple of years and joined the Air Force.

That may not seem like the typical employment choice for one who is deeply attached to the great outdoors, but it worked for him.

Before he retired as a major after 13 years of service, Dale wrangled an extended series of assignments in Europe where he was able to spend some high old times schussing about the Alps as an avid Alpine skier.

Already an experienced back-packer and sports parachutist in his college days, he became a paragliding enthusiast while in the Air Force.

"When I signed up, I never intended to stay in for more than the four years I was committed to, but I kept getting one good job after another, and it just kind of happened," says Dale.

The fun ended when he was assigned to NATO after the Berlin Wall came down and, "I was bored to tears," he says.

That's when he retired, but his affinity for the sports he mastered in the military stayed with him, along with the jingle in Dale's pockets from his retirement pay.

He headed for Crested Butte, Colorado where he purchased a paragliding company, and for a while there it looked like the two might never be reunited.

Dale admits that although he frequently thought of his old college flame, he was reluctant to contact her during his service years since "many were not big fans of the military in those days."

When he finally screwed up his courage and wrote to

Debbie eight years after their last contact, he assumed his reluctance was justified since he received no response.

It turned out that an erroneous address given to him by a secretary at the University of Alabama, rather than disinterest, caused the delay. The letter with the outdated address took months to reach her while being forwarded from one place to another.

Once she finally received it, Debbie responded immediately, and Dale was delighted, though somewhat surprised, to learn she shared his enthusiasm for rekindling that budding romance of bygone years.

After a flurry of correspondence, they started getting together, taking turns visiting between Crested Butte and Tybee, where Debbie established her residence while working with the Georgia Mental Health Department in 1982.

Dale Williams and Debbie Kearney discuss the many things they have in common.

Debbie, who says she was lured to Savannah because of a now long-dead "relationship," continued to embrace the area despite the demise of the beau thing.

"I lost a relationship, but I found a home, found my niche," she says. "I have the coastal area."

"It was a lot tougher on me going to Tybee," laughs Dale.

"Coming down to sea level from 9,000 feet wreaks havoc with your hemoglobin count.

"It takes at least two weeks to acclimate again, and when I went back and started climbing up those mountains, I'd be gasping for breath. I'd be cussing Savannah on the side of a mountain in Colorado. Going the other way was not that big a deal for Debbie."

During her years on Tybee, Debbie took up sea kayaking and became devoted to the sport.

Dale had exposed her to paragliding, which she says was a "thrilling experience," and she couldn't wait to introduce him to the new sport (strictly speaking, sea kayaking is not "new" since the craft from which it evolved was used by Innuits on Greenland and Aleuts in the Aleutians thousands of years ago to travel great distances over water), but it is a relatively new sport here and was a brand new activity for Dale.

He was smitten with the sport immediately, and now they had one more thing in common.

That proved more than enough to push them into what seemed a preordained union.

They agreed to settle on Tybee after their marriage because Debbie loved the place and had a long-established practice here.

In addition, they were anxious to permanently cement their relationship after such an inordinate delay, and the nature of her job would have required a year's notification for her to leave.

The thought of postponing the knot tying and togetherness until she could join him in Colorado was intolerable.

Besides, Dale believed, and had repeatedly proven, he can make it any place where there's an outdoors and was confident because, "I had a lifetime of experiences to call upon."

Although he was captivated by Colorado's mountains, he found he was equally attracted to the Georgia coast.

"The thing about the scenery in Crested Butte is that it was always right there in your face," he says. "It's there all the time. There's nothing subtle about it. Georgia's coast is just as beautiful. It's just more subtle. It's horizontal here, and you have to see things much more close up."

"In Crested Butte you would look out and see for 60 miles. Here you look out for 60, or maybe 600 yards. Climbing the lighthouse is about as vertical as you can get."

But paragliding, which has superseded hang gliding for birdman wannabes, since the chutes can be folded into a backpack for the hike up to launch areas, is pretty much alien to the East where there are a few glide areas in the densely forested Smokies.

"And you need updrafts from the valley floors coming

up the mountains" for proper paragliding, says Dale, noting that there are few high hills or dunes, save for those in Kitty Hawk, North Carolina, on the coast to provide such conditions.

Dale says parasailing, where one is pulled by and tethered to boat and unable to climb or maneuver, is totally different from paragliding.

His highest vertical lift from launch on a paraglide was 6,000 feet, and his longest flight lasted four-and-a-half hours.

"It would have lasted much longer, but I was limited by my bladder," he laughs.

After being introduced to sea kayaks by Debbie, Dale found he had a new sport of choice which was far more appropriate for his new location.

"It's the perfect sport for the Georgia coast," he says.

Dale discusses kayak business.

Dale soon became totally immersed in sea kayaking, reading all the literature available on the subject, taking lessons from experts, watching videos, and kayaking in coastal waters from South Carolina to Florida.

"I had more fun during the first months I was here than I can remember anywhere," says Dale.

He says the difference between sea kayaks and those designed for white water is that the latter are shorter and have rounded bottoms for maneuverability in rock-filled streams while sea kayaks have planing hulls, track better, and are far faster in open water.

"Sea kayaking has everything," he says. "It has fluidity, speed, and motion, and you can absolutely relax. It can be low adrenaline, where you don't watch the weather, or you can go out and 'shred' in the big pre-hurricane waves."

Word spread about his devotion to and growing knowledge of the sport and ultimately reached the owners of a kayak company in Savannah who had grown tired of the business.

Dale was ripe for a new occupation and, like his and Debbie's, this seemed to be a perfect marriage, so he acquired the business and all its equipment two years ago.

His purchase was propitious. Sea kayaking has now become the fastest growing non-powered water sport in the country.

After acquiring the business, he expanded it under a new name, Sea Kayak Georgia.

Not only has the inventory of kayaks been increased to the point where there are more than enough to handle all his clients' needs, but training programs, including navigational skills, day outings, and extended kayak camping expeditions have multiplied.

Those new to the sport need training because it seems so easy, "since nine out of 10 times it is, and people get a false sense of security about what skills they really need," observes Debbie.

"Worse yet," says Dale, "because newcomers have had no training, they are overly cautious, so what they allow themselves to do in a sea kayak is extremely limited."

Dale washes down the kayaks at Sea Kayak Georgia.

"By gaining knowledge and understanding about what the challenges are, they can prepare for them and do things that were conceptually way beyond their limits."

The main thing to learn is how to get back into the boat when you're completely out of it, he says, noting that basic kayak lessons last about three hours but vary depending on how athletic a person is, "and the learning process can go on for a lifetime."

The need for navigational skills becomes apparent when one is just a couple of miles off shore.

"It's a real challenge to set a course for a channel marker when an island becomes just barely a blob on the horizon from where you're sitting just two-and-a-half feet above the water," says Dale. "You can be totally dependent on your compass if there's any kind of overcast."

Dale offers kayak camping excursions annually in Maine, where he and Debbie generally take their vacation voyages, as well as Florida and along the entire coast of Georgia.

He claims his company now offers more high-level instruction and extended camping trips than any other on the East Coast because most others emphasize lower-level instruction and day trips.

Dale oversees the entire outdoor program for Wilderness Southeast, a non-profit organization promoting environmental stewardship.

Because this position takes so much of his time, and Wilderness Southeast has recently changed its direction, Dale says they will end their relationship in the near future.

Dale has seven qualified kayak instructors on his staff, including Debbie, who helps out with teaching occasionally and says, "I love it!"

He has just initiated a workshop, in which educators

from clubs as far away as the Great Lakes and Maine are participating, to provide accreditation for instructors to instruct instructors, and plans to make it an annual event.

Looking to the future, he sees broader horizons, including opening a kayak store to handle sales and centralize operations, and taking trips much farther afield.

This summer he and Debbie plan to forsake their annual kayak trip to Maine for one along the west coast of Scotland, and if things go as well as they anticipate,

Dale and Debbie display one of their sea kayaks.

similar excursions may be offered to Dale's clients.

Now it seems Debbie and Dale have virtually everything in common except their last names.

Debbie says she kept Kearney as her last name when they married because she had utilized it in her business for so long.

Even their names have found a common chord in the family, however, since both have been bestowed upon their 4-year-old daughter.

Her name is Emily Kearney-Williams and, yes, she's already into kayaks which have become another common thread for this family.

POSTSCRIPT: Dale and Debbie remain on Tybee and are "still sitting at the same spot at that same table" in their "funky ol' beach house... wouldn't have it any other way," according to Dale. They made that trip to Scotland which he says was "one of the most memorable of our lives" and led to his creation of instructor certification programs to sea kayaking locations in Ireland, Wales, Alaska, Chile, and China as well as across the U.S. Dale sold Sea Kayak Georgia about 15 years ago and now operates Sea Kayaking USA, while Debbie continues with her psychotherapy. Their daughter, Emily, was in Alaska several years ago when she met the man to whom she is now engaged. They plan to marry in 2023.

Bonnie Gaster -

Covering the Island With Smiles

Helping Her Way To Success

She's celebrating her 50th anniversary on the island she's played a key role in developing for 25 years.

Bonnie Gaster, an omnipresent, peripatetic bundle of energy who darts about Tybee and adjacent islands from early mornings until late at night, hasn't lost a step in those years, despite the thousands of miles she's covered.

Bonnie, who seems to have been born with a smile on her face, has probably sold more residential real estate in Savannah and nearby islands than any of the myriad purveyors of property who have come and gone over the years.

She handled more than 120 transactions last year and has averaged 80 annually for the past five years.

Much of her success is based on the pleasure she derives from her profession and her genuine desire to ensure that both sellers and buyers "are happy with the deal."

And while income is important, it's not the sole reason she is in it. She's been known to slash or eliminate her commission completely to get the right people into the right residence.

"I've never let my commission get in the way of making a sale," she says. "I'm not pushing development. This is my home, and I want the right people here."

Bonnie says she knows almost immediately whether a person is "right for Tybee. They either love it immediately and fit right in, or they don't like the island at all."

She looks on her clients as part of her extended island family.

"Tybee's really a feeling," she says. "It's not for everybody. You don't sit on the fence when you come here. But if you love it, you love it! I've had people come down for the first time who don't even want to go back to get their belongings!"

She also spends considerable time helping new real estate agents get to know Tybee, even though they are her competitors. "It's good for our island," she says.

The bulk of her sales come from references volunteered by satisfied customers, and she considers her job to be that of a facilitator.

"There are times that you cannot make something happen, but there are times when you can modify a deal where everyone is happy," she says. "Real estate is one industry where everything is negotiable."

Despite her success, Bonnie is self-effacing about her

Bonnie Gaster discusses her career.

prowess in this highly competitive field.

Typical of her desire to maintain a low profile and her concern that someone might be offended should they think she is being singled out for special treatment, she was extremely reluctant to be the subject of this column.

Bonnie is a very special lady.

She has been involved in numerous community service activities, efforts to help fellow residents, and general island boosterism. Numerous Tybee residents who have been touched by her generosity have suggested that she deserves special recognition.

Bonnie has served as a director with the Savannah Board of Realtors and is particularly active on that organization's Realtors Political Action Committee, for which she raises funds each year by sponsoring special events.

She seems willing to go to any extreme to help any cause that benefits the island.

Once, Mayor Walter Parker enlisted her to help organize an art exhibit at City Hall and she was given less than six weeks to pull the project off.

Bonnie arranged to borrow a bunch of old school blackboards, draped them with white material and hung paintings on them when planners were stumped as to how to display the artwork.

In addition to the inside exhibit, she had bands and a number of food concessions set up outside.

"The biggest problem we had was all the extension cords for the food booths and musicians," she says. "We'd blow the power every time something else was plugged in, and every time the waste treatment pump station kicked in, all the electricity went out."

At one point when power was lost, Bonnie and a friend crawled under the musicians' stage to readjust the electrical hookups.

"All you could see were our behinds sticking up in front of the stage as we crawled under it," she laughs. "But it was wonderful. We had 5,000 people there."

Bonnie, a twin whose brother died in childbirth, weighed only a pound and a half when she was born in Sandford, North Carolina.

She was given the name Bonnie Barbara Brewer ("You try to say that fast," she laughs. "It was impossible for a kid!") and brought to the island by her parents when she was just one day over a year old.

She laments the fact that they did not bring her two days earlier because "if I'd been brought here the day before my birthday. I could have been a native. Now I've got to do my 99 years like the rest of 'em to earn that designation."

The family resided on Chimney Pot Creek where her father was a mechanic and cabinetmaker. Her family also operated a small RV park, several rental units, and an antique shop.

Bonnie rambled through the dunes, frollicked among the waves, and cavorted about the old pavilion with the handful of other kids who resided on the island as a child.

"Chief McCutcheon (the police chief at the time) taught us to swim in the ocean beside the pier," she recalls. "And if I had a dollar for every time I fell on my butt at the pavilion skating rink ,I probably wouldn't be working now. The surface was wavy from the weathering and had nail heads sticking up all over it."

She says the only trouble she got into as a child was when she failed to tell her mother she had gone down to the creek to go crabbing or over to the railroad tracks to pick plums.

Bonnie attended St. Michael's Catholic School on Tybee.

"There were only five of us in my first-grade class, and I got blamed for everything," she laughs.

"Jay Buckley sat behind me, and when I turned around to slap him for pulling my hair, I would get caught."

"Thelma Barfield sat in front of me and talked all the time, but she had this angelic look about her, and when Sister Mary Carolyn came by, it was my ear she would grab. That's why this ear (Bonnie tugs at her right ear) is so much longer than the other one. Sister was always pulling on it."

Bonnie smiles as usual in her Tybee home.

Bonnie remembers playing in mud puddles in the middle of Meddin Drive at Fort Screven when it was considered a high traffic day if a single car passed by in an hour.

"The biggest problem we had was when our dog chased the garbage men," she says, noting that prisoners were used as trash collectors at that time.

She says her world was pretty much confined to Tybee until she finished elementary school since "everything we did was on the island, and that was great."

The only time her family left the island was to go into town occasionally to shop for things that were not available on Tybee.

Then she went to high school in Savannah.

"I didn't know we were poor until then," she laughs. "Oh, maybe we weren't really poor, but we didn't have a lot of material things. We had things you couldn't put a price tag on."

"But when I started school in Savannah, all the girls wore a different pair of shoes every day. It was something! My father believed you needed only two pair of shoes, one for church and one for school."

"I remember after I started school in the city, I really wanted a pair of T-strapped shoes (which were the rage in 1958). Dad said I didn't need them."

Following high school, Bonnie attended the University of Georgia where she studied pharmacy.

She says she never pursued a career in pharmacy "because I knew it wasn't for me. I couldn't be penned in, and I didn't have the discipline."

After graduating she returned to Tybee where she met her future husband, Ray Gaster.

He was a helicopter pilot stationed at Hunter Airfield but was living in a beachfront house with two buddies, one of whom was introduced to Bonnie by her mother.

Once she met the others, it was Ray she became enamored of. They married when she was 21, then moved into Savannah where they restored a historic house on Gordon Street and had three children.

It was in Savannah that Bonnie first entered the realty business back in 1973 and wound up working with three different firms for almost 20 years.

Jackie Horne, her first broker, was instrumental in establishing her sound footing in sales techniques.

"Don't ever say they won't take it, and don't ever say you'll never get it," are the basic tenets she taught, says Bonnie.

The premise is that what a piece of property is worth is what a willing buyer and a willing seller are willing to settle for, and the secret is to be creative and to "know the money market" and have a good knowledge of how to finance property, she says.

Her early days in real estate sales were not all roses and picket fences.

Bonnie recalls when she was initially hired to sell property at The Landings on Skidaway Island, where she later moved, male members of her firm tried hard to intimidate her.

"When I started at The Landings, there were only five houses for sale, and I had to learn to be a 'dirt' salesman. I was their 'token' woman and some of the guys tried to scare me to death," she recalls.

"The second day I was there, one man brought me a snake bite kit, and a few days later he brought a chemical ice kit explaining that when I got bitten, I should put it on the wound rather than cut around the bite and try to suck the poison out. I had nightmares for weeks!"

The men "felt that they should be out there stomping the bushes," she says, noting that she was thinking about leaving when another salesman befriended her, assuaging her concerns by having her don boots and jeans for a walk around the undeveloped property.

"We literally walked every available lot that was there. He said the first thing you want to do if you think a snake is there is to let it know you're not afraid of it. Make some noise and talk a little louder, and I learned."

Although her male associates tried to convince her the area was infested with them, Bonnie says she saw only one snake during her tenure with the firm, and both she and the snake quickly parted company.

Bonnie continued her sales efforts on Skidaway for 13 years, during which time she was responsible for bringing in about 600 families.

She attributes her sales success to her "gift of direction," which enabled her to know where a person needed to place a house for the proper exposure, and her ability to consider resale possibilities when selling property.

"You never know when someone buys with the intention of staying forever if something will change," she says, noting that she always tries to set things up so that her clients can get out without suffering financial loss if they're forced to sell shortly after purchasing property.

After her mother passed away in 1977, Bonnie says she was reluctant to visit Tybee for years, fearing that "it wouldn't feel right."

She finally returned to the island to help a customer in 1983.

"It was like a weight was lifted from my shoulders when I reached the top of Lazaretto Creek Bridge," she says. "I had a big sigh of relief. It was like I had been denying myself access to Tybee, and now I was finally home again. I found out I needed to be on Tybee."

Following her divorce, Bonnie made her permanent return to the beach when she purchased property on 19th Street with two friends.

The trio not only lived on the property but developed it, renovating and selling the main house, then building three duplexes and selling the units they didn't occupy.

Bonnie was off and running in Tybee real estate, and she's never stopped.

Bonnie beside some of the "stuff" she collects.

She does take a break occasionally to acquire bargain priced pieces to add to her growing array of collectible "stuff."

She likes old things and has a collection of antique bottles, Depression Glass, McCoy pottery, and other "pick up stuff" on display in her marsh-side home.

While her sales have always been prodigious, staying at the top of her game wasn't always easy with three children in tow.

Bonnie remembers her guilt feelings when a neighbor described a back yard conversation between her two daughters, Amy and Carrie, when Carrie was role playing as her mother and said:

"Be quiet now! I'm on the phone and I have to go. I have to show a house!"

"Boy, does that make you feel bad," she says of the recollection, admitting that it was a fair assessment of her life in real estate.

She is constantly on the telephone, in her home, in her car enroute to appointments, or while she is attempting to eat or show property. The phone is like an appendage that rings incessantly.

"Sometimes it felt like the children were being raised by a committee" since friends were always pitching in to help when she was busy with sales, says Bonnie.

"I remember once when the office got a call from the school saying her son Michael wanted another hamburger for lunch (children were then given a dollar to buy lunch at school). Clark Honnold answered and said 'well let him have one. We'll send a dollar over later'."

Bonnie says when she stopped by the office, she found a dollar bill stuck on the message board with a note signed "Designated parent for the day."

On another occasion, Michael, then 6, was riding the bus back to her office after school and got off at the wrong stop. Discovering his mistake as the bus pulled off, he chased it down the street and was near exhaustion when a kindly female motorist stopped and picked him up.

Michael was able to give her directions to his mother's office, and she delivered him safely.

"Things can be tough for a working mother," says Bonnie.

She and her children successfully survived the ordeal, however.

"All three are now grown and successful, and all are still living in the area," says Bonnie with pride.

Her daughter, Amy, was married not long ago in a "surprise" ceremony on the deck overlooking the water behind Bonnie's Eagles Nest home.

Amy and her fiancé, Darryl Wise, had planned to be married in Scotland, but the logistics of arranging the ceremony by long distance became difficult, and they opted to marry at her mother's house at what the 75 people in attendance thought was a birthday party.

The guests were eating barbecue and partying when Amy and Darryl slipped upstairs and changed into semi-formal attire, then returned to the strains of "The Wedding March."

"Surprise!" the family screamed in unison as the couple emerged on the deck to say their vows while standing barefoot on rocks imported from Scotland which had been presented as a wedding gift.

The ceremony took place as the setting sun was reflected at high tide on Chimney Pot Creek.

"There wasn't a dry eye in the crowd," says Bonnie. "It was perfect!"

Bonnie worked her way through some slow times in property sales on Tybee during the late 1980s, but she was always optimistic about the island's development.

"Things really started to boom in the early '90s and they're getting better all the time," she says.

"I remember last year I started to get calls in late January after the dead season over the holidays. This year the phone started ringing on the weekend after Christmas! I had five appointments on the Saturday following Christmas."

Even though her sales are soaring, Bonnie is quick to assert that she is not pushing development for development's sake.

"Our small island business community needs permanent residents to survive," she says.

"They stay open for us in the winter, but their summer business is what enables them to survive. We all pray for good weather on Memorial Day, the Fourth of July, and Labor Day. That's when they make enough to carry them through the winter."

Bonnie says many people have the mistaken impression that there is almost no land left to develop on Tybee, "but that's not true. We have a lot of vacant land here and there that can be built on."

Bonnie looks over deck of her house in Eagles Nest where daughter Amy was married.

She thinks the belief that little land is left may have helped recent real estate sales since people are rushing to buy, thinking that soon nothing will be left.

Bonnie hopes Tybee will retain its gregarious nature

and remain basically as it is in the future, "but you have to have some change, and I want it to be an orderly change. There needs to be consistency and responsibility in development. There has to be a compromise."

She is a proponent of moderating the island's height limitations on buildings, but "it's not because I'm pushing development, which is what people accuse me of," she says.

"It's a fairness issue. People forget that the 35-foot limit was originally set in 1971 because of fire safety. Our fire truck ladders would only reach that high. That was all right before the FEMA regulations were applied in 1978."

Until that time, you could build three stories of living space starting at ground level, but with FEMA requiring houses to be 14 feet above sea level, they must now be built on pilings since the island's average elevation is only seven feet above sea level.

"Living space" construction now starts at eight feet above ground level in most cases since most lots tend to be so small that off-street parking must be provided under new houses, reducing living space to two levels rather than three.

With the increasing cost of land on the island requiring newcomers to spend more for less living space than their predecessors, Bonnie thinks it's unfair to maintain the 35-foot height limitation.

At same time, she opposes continuing the variances granted by City Council permitting structures to exceed height regulations.

"I think we ought to take the highest building currently on the island and cut it off there," she says. "If one person has the right to build that high, everyone should. After all, Georgia is a property rights state."

Her hope is that the height limit would be set at the highest structure in commercial and residential areas and that no variances be permitted for anything above those heights.

If you want to discuss this issue or anything else about real estate on the island, you'll find Bonnie dashing about Tybee on either a mission of mercy or to show property.

She'll be the lady with the sparkling smile and the phone glued to her ear.

POSTSCRIPT: Bonnie Gaster retired in 2018 after 48 years in the real estate business. She is now living at Harmony at Savannah, an independent and assisted living facility, but says "my heart is still on Tybee. When you get that sand between your toes you never want to leave." Bonnie says she believes she's had "the best of all lives," and still feels good at age 76 after surviving breast cancer for 22 years. She laughed recently when she recalled a friend "told me I was too mean to die."

Freddie Grotheer - Octogenarian Still Going Strong

Renaissance Man Thrives On Tybee

He does a mean tap dance, paints prolifically, plays in a popular band, serves as pianist for a monthly dinner group, and plans to perform weekends at the Tybee Arts Association Lighthouse Gallery.

That's a pretty hectic schedule for a man in his prime.

Frederick ("Freddie") Martine Grotheer, a dapper entertainer/artist who celebrated his birthday in July in conjunction with the Grotheer family reunion at his Back River home, is just hitting his stride.

It was his 89th birthday, and the likes of this 89-year-old you will rarely see.

Like Grandma Moses, he started painting seriously only late in life, actually far later than that famous lady. Freddie got serious about art after moving to Tybee when he was 86.

He claims the clean ocean air has rejuvenated him and

given him his voluminous artistic endeavors and other interests, who can argue?

Freddie says he's heard of people who came to Tybee "with arthritis so bad they had to crawl across the beach to the water, but after a while they could walk."

Freddie Grotheer and a young friend celebrate at party in Tybee's Memorial Park.

He believes the island has miraculous healing powers, citing his own renewed energy.

"I just can't stop painting and drawing now!" he says. "I get up in the middle of the night. I have so many ideas, so many things I want to paint. I'm at it all the time!"

His work is familiar to most island residents and sells rapidly at outlets such as the Lighthouse Gallery, Captain Chris' Restaurant on Butler Avenue, and the TAG Arts and Antique Center on U.S. 80.

Freddie has just been named "Artist of the Month" for August by the Arts Association. It was based on his popular gallery performance at a special "Sizzling Summer" show there in mid-July that he was invited to entertain gallery patrons every Sunday afternoon.

He illustrated his impressive talent at the show by not only exhibiting his art but playing both the keyboard and "washtub bass," drawing caricatures of those in attendance, and regaling the crowd with an impromptu tap dance.

Freddie is an unabashed showman who plays piano for the Tuesday Dinner Group's regular gathering in the Tybee Light Shrine Club. He also performs with the popular Crabettes Band, dancing and plunking his unusual one-string bass.

But while he has created a large number of paintings which are highly coveted by admirers, you can pretty much forget about acquiring one.

Freddie doesn't like to part with his paintings. He

keeps his originals at home where they surround him like old friends he just can't bid good-bye to.

He normally sells only prints of his work, but badgered by numerous requests, he recently painted a copy of one of those originals.

It depicts a soothing Back River sunset which he placed in the TAG store where it was snapped up immediately. (You can find it at my house on the island. Viewings are available for a small fee: a smile and a modicum of small talk. For an extra smile you can see a caricature he created of me and a friend.)

Freddie learned to play his washtub bass when a buddy built it for him almost a half century ago.

He already played the piano, becoming interested in that instrument when his daughter, Linda Larsen, whose house he now shares, was taking lessons as a child.

He quickly learned to play and read music, and Linda discontinued her lessons after deciding she'd never play as well as her father because he made it look so easy.

Freddie also played the harmonica and had a yen to join in local "jam" sessions but figured they had enough of those and keyboards.

That's when his washtub bass building friend decided this was the instrument for Freddie.

He proved prophetic.

Freddie was soon producing the full range of regular bass sounds on the unusual single-string instrument

Freddie works on drawing of Belinda McLain and J.R. Roseberry.

while making this look easy as well.

He says it looks so easy that the people approach him constantly asking to try it since it seems so simple anyone could play the thing.

They soon discover that looks are deceiving. It's harder to play than it is to stay dry at Tybee's annual Beach Bum Parade.

The instrument consists of a steel string anchored at one end through the center of the bottom of an old metal washtub with soft rubber pads beneath the hole back of which the string is tied. The other end is attached to the top of a bamboo pole with a slotted bottom which is placed on the rim of the turned over tub.

Freddie places the bamboo pole just below his ear, pressing it against the left side of his neck while keeping one foot on the wash tub.

"I can feel the vibrations, and I just know what notes I need and how to find them," he says.

Those notes are produced by altering tension on the string by bending or releasing pressure on the pole while fingering up and down the string.

Freddie was so good just after he started playing the instrument that he and some buddies were booked into the Elks Club to play.

That's when he learned he needed to join the musicians' union if he planned to play professionally.

"A guy at the union office laughed when he saw the washtub and said I couldn't get in playing that thing," recalls Freddie.

Freddie plays unusual single string bass.

The union secretary intervened, however, saying that if people wanted to pay to hear Freddie play it, he was qualified to join.

In later years, when country music was overtaken by jazz in Savannah, Freddie bought a standard upright bass to go with the flow.

But his cart preceded his horse by a Mark McGwire homer.

He placed placards around town advertising live band entertainment, and almost before he hung the last of them, he was booked into the Moose Club.

Freddie says he had a small problem. He had not yet formed his band.

But that didn't stop him. He called several friends, including a top-flight guitarist, and the group showed up to perform even though they had never practiced together.

That wasn't their most discordant note, however. Freddie had that brand new bass, but he had not learned to play it.

The guitarist's solution was "to play his guitar real loud to cover me while I faked it," laughs Freddie.

That worked until the club manager approached Freddie during a break complaining that the guitarist was playing too loud and demanding that Freddie have him reduce his volume.

They limped through the rest of the night, and before his next booking Freddie had mastered his new instrument.

His pickup jazz group called themselves "The Commandos" and remained popular in the area for a number of years.

Still, Freddie claims that he can get more music and a wider range of sounds from the old wash tub, which he claims is his instrument of choice.

While an accomplished musician, music was not his forte during his early life in Savannah, where he was born and raised, the son of German immigrant parents who owned a grocery store on Drayton Street.

During World War I, the Grotheers fled to New York by steamer because they were ostracized in Savannah.

"No one would buy anything in my father's store because he was German," says Freddie, who was in the second grade at the time.

When they returned to Savannah, the family lived temporarily in the White Bluff area and it was there that Freddie, at age 11, first exhibited his extraordinary talent as an artist.

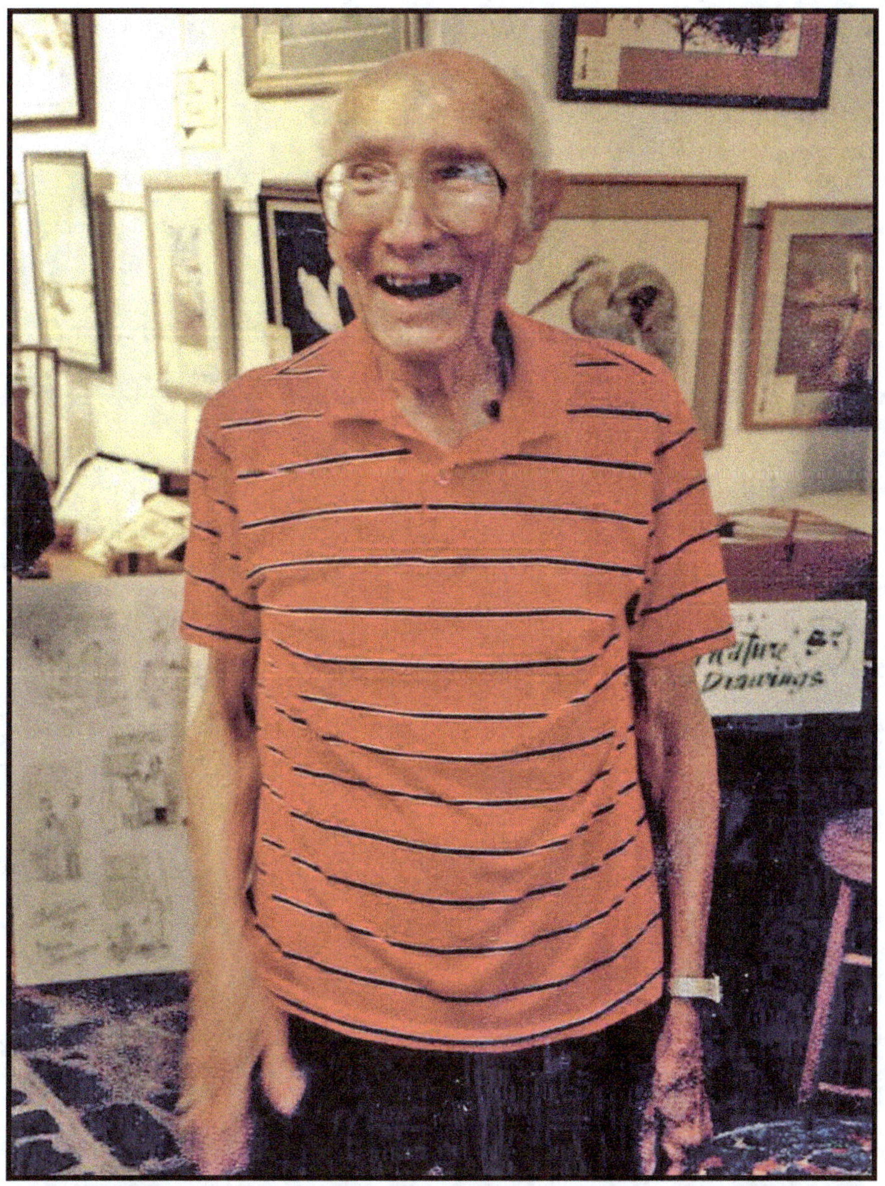

Freddie smiles while describing art in his studio.

He created an oil painting of the farmhouse beside a pond where they lived, revealing remarkable ability for an artist of his years.

Freddie had completely forgotten about the painting

until it was presented to him on his birthday/reunion in July by the descendants of the owners of the White Bluff house his family had rented.

"I didn't realize I was that good back then," he says, while admiring the painting now on display in his home.

Freddie says he wasn't into music during his Savannah school days and wasn't much of a student either, dropping out for lack of interest.

What he could do very well was draw, a talent his mother recognized immediately, sending him to work for his brother who operated a poster-making shop off Broughton Street.

Freddie proved so adept at poster designs that she insisted he attend art classes at Pratt Institute in New York to hone his skills.

He excelled there and, while still 18, was hired by Republic Engraving Co. to produce artwork and create rubber molds which were used to print his designs on bags and other packaging paraphernalia.

Tiring of New York after several years, he turned down a job offer from Pratt and returned to Savannah.

"You know, I never did ask them what the job was," says Freddie. "I kind of wished I had, but that would probably have changed my whole life!"

Freddie was employed by Dixie Engraving Co. in Savannah, again creating rubber printing molds until that firm reduced its staff.

After leaving Dixie, he accepted a position with Republic Engraving in Chicago, and asked his girlfriend, Brunell, who lived in Savannah, to join him.

Freddie married the woman he called "Nell" just after she arrived in the Windy City in the late 1930s.

The newlyweds returned to Savannah shortly thereafter, driving down in their sparkling new Chevrolet with its spare tires mounted in fender wells on each side.

"It was really classy," he smiles.

Freddie was hired by Mente Bag Co., where he created designs for croaker sacks, before being lured away by Union Bag when it first began operations in Savannah.

"They made me an offer I couldn't refuse, with paid vacation and all," he recalls.

Freddie was still working there at the beginning of World War II.

"That's when I told Nell I was not going to be drafted; that I was going to get in the war right away by enlisting," he says.

Freddie chose the Marines, attending boot camp at nearby Parris Island, before joining a First Marine Amphibious Corps unit in New Caledonia, then shipping out immediately for Guadalcanal, where they arrived just after the island was secured.

"But the Japs were still around," says Freddie. "They were so hungry they came in to stand in our chow line."

And it wasn't long before he was in the thick of the

action in the Pacific.

He says he was assigned to an unusual unit consisting of only 75 men with a full colonel in charge.

"We were surprised to learn we had such a high-ranking officer for such a small outfit, and then we heard it was a 'suicide' unit and wondered how we got in it" since no one had volunteered, he says.

The group assembled sound equipment with huge speakers they were ordered to install on Bougainville, the largest island in the Solomons, just before the invasion there.

"We were taken to Bougainville by PT boats, then we loaded the stuff in rubber boats and hauled it ashore," he says. "The whole operation had to be carried out on a dark night so the Japanese wouldn't spot us."

The Marines were armed only with carbines which Freddie says would not have provided sufficient firepower for a real battle.

"The idea was that nobody was going to survive or all of us would," he says.

The first problem they encountered was Japanese snipers hidden atop palm trees who could pin down their entire unit.

A single Marine was designated to head out through the trees to draw sniper fire so the other men could locate them.

"Once a sniper fired, we'd spot him and shoot him down, but I was glad I wasn't the one who had to walk out there first!" says Freddie.

After eliminating the snipers, the Marines installed the sound equipment, floated a lighted balloon tethered to a string high above, and slipped back to the waiting PT boats.

The sound equipment was wired with explosives to blow up after a fixed amount of time but while it lasted, it blasted out all the sounds of an invasion, and the lighted balloon looked like the lights of a large ship from a distance.

The ploy convinced the Japanese an invasion was underway and sent their troops to the spot while the real invasion took place elsewhere.

"I think they may have used the same trick during the Iraq invasion since they fooled them into thinking they were attacking at one spot while they went in at another place," says Freddie.

His entire unit survived the operation.

Bougainville was captured early in 1944 and Freddie's unit was rotated back to the United States where he spent most of the remainder of the war in military hospitals undergoing treatment for a severe case of malaria he contracted in the Pacific.

After his discharge, he returned to his job at Union Bag, but soon decided to go into business for himself.

"I increased my salary the first month," says Freddie of his firm, which designed printing molds and prepared commercial art for newspapers, posters, and billboards.

"Another company offered me $20,000 a year to join them, and that convinced me I wasn't charging enough," he grins. "I figured out the $20,000 meant they would be paying me $25 an hour so that's what I started charging, then upped it to $31."

That was definitely not small potatoes in the 1950s, when most folks were earning $40 a week.

One measure of his success was his purchase of houses in both Savannah and on Tybee, where he and Nell spent their weekends.

"We were crazy about the beach, and I always loved coming out, but when the kids came, they didn't seem to care for it, so we sold the place after a while," he says.

The family later moved to Windsor Forest, but Freddie says the air there left something to be desired.

"We'd get mildew in the house, and you would breathe that stuff, and it was really bad for you," he says. "I kept breathing that stuff in and I got pneumonia two times. It was terrible!"

After Freddie suffered a heart attack when he was in his 80s, he retired, and he and Nell moved to a house on Tybee's beach front.

"The air here is so pure!" he says. "You've got thousands of miles out over the ocean, and there's nothing to pollute it. Ships are all that's out there."

He thinks the surrounding salt marsh is also conducive to good health.

"They've got sulfur in them, and Little Tybee is full of sulfur, and they use that in medicine," he says.

Freddie performs at birthday celebration.

Although Nell passed away shortly after their arrival, Freddie says his own health has constantly improved.

"It's a miracle!" he exclaims. "My body and mind don't feel that old, and I'm doing more than ever. The doctor here asked me what I was taking I'm in such good shape."

"I think it's the air and all the things I'm doing. It's good exercise, and exercise makes your heart stronger. All those people out exercising now have the right idea."

Freddie sold his beachfront house just after Nell's death and moved into the ground-level portion of his daughter's home.

He says he gave the money from the proceeds of his house sale and some additional funds to Linda and her sister, who bought a house in Savannah.

"Why wait until you die to do those things?" he asks. "If you do it now, you can see things happen. Otherwise, you don't."

Freddie says he plans to remain here "forever. I've been thinking about what I want to do in the future. I'd like to keep things as they are if time could just stand still."

The only thing missing is Nell, he says.

"I really do miss her terrible. I find myself crying sometimes thinking of the things I could've done and didn't do. It's her memory I'm living with. I don't want to live with some other woman. I don't have any need for anyone else."

"Besides, I'm a firm believer in the Hereafter, and she's only been gone a short time. We're going to be together soon and I don't want Nell to ask who this other woman was when I get together with her again."

POSTSCRIPT: Freddie Grotheer, who always remained true to his beloved Nell, passed away not long after this was written.

Espy Geissler-

Hunter House Chef is Much More

Artist,
Musician,
Raconteur

Talk about your Renaissance men! Tybee's got 'em.

Espy's one.

Espy Geissler, the co-owner and principal chef of Hunter House, Tybee's most acclaimed restaurant, is a musician, an artist, a chef, and an entrepreneur.

When relatively well lubricated late nights at local watering holes, he casually discusses the work of such diverse writers as Carl Jung, Richard Brautigan, e.e. cummings, Kurt Vonnegut, Lewis Grizzard and others with insights which escape most casual readers.

Espy has been into art and music since he was a child in Savannah, where he attended Pape School, the predecessor of Country Day School, and made frequent trips to Tybee with his family.

He's studied harmonica under, and performed professionally with, some of the country's leading blues musicians.

He's also sold hundreds of his paintings and once had his own art studio in Atlanta while displaying his work in shows both there and in Manhattan.

Along the way, he studied the culinary arts under a noted French chef in New York, learning to appreciate and prepare exotic cuisine.

But it will take you awhile to ferret out such stuff.

Unlike more garrulous types who inundate you instantly with their unsolicited verbal autobiographies, then lapse into agonizingly boring repetition, Espy creeps up on you. Like eating an artichoke, you peel off a leaf at a time, savoring each one slowly, until you finally get to the heart of the matter.

Your initial impression is that he's just another latter-day hippie...a tall, thin, slightly stooped man wearing a grungy T-shirt and shorts and sporting a graying mustache and a pony tail tied behind his neck with a rubber band.

Espy is unobtrusive, but he seems to know a lot of people, all of whom apparently like him and seem drawn to him to engage in extended conversations despite the crush of raucous, ear-numbing crowds in the beach bars he regularly frequents.

After hearing him expound on Jung's concept of the four quadrants of the mind; the difference between European and American thought processes; "believing in your heart" as opposed to general knowledge; and how he's developed a deeper understanding of these over the years, you want to hear more.

Prodding gently, peeling back the leaves, you learn Espy is a native Savannahian from a well-heeled family who has spent most of his life studying, working, playing with, and assimilating knowledge from experts in numerous unrelated fields.

He started playing the harmonica at age 15 when he was given one by a friend.

"I just loved it," he says. "It has a kind of lonesome sound, and if you wanted to play something on it, you could. And you could make different sounds. You could make it sound like an organ or a guitar, a single note instrument.

"I fooled with it and fooled with it, and I learned it's not that simple. I bought all of these blues albums and played with them. I was beating my brains out, but I was getting fairly good.

"Then I met Steve Miller (a noted musician then performing in Atlanta), and he sat me down on the steps of an apartment building and said, 'you need to get a little resonance going, some space to play in,' and he showed me how to tighten my lips up and how to breathe while I played, and I got better."

About this time Espy met Buddy "Fatty" Moss, an elderly black blues musician, and started going to Moss's house, listening to his stories while they both drank too much vodka.

He performed with Moss for the next five years, playing at all black blues joints in Atlanta.

One of his favorite memories of those days occurred in

one of those dimly lit bistros.

"I was the only white guy there. I was young, and Buddy would buy me beers and take care of me," Espy recalls. "It was a rough joint."

"One night it just got weird. Moss was playing real primitive blues, switching around in the middle of the thing and I just couldn't figure out what he was doin'. I was playin' so hard I had blood coming out of the corners of my mouth, and I asked, 'Fatty, what key are you playin' in man?' He just looked at me and said: 'Boy, don't worry about what key it's in, you just play what you're posed to play'. I'll never forget it. From that time on I've just played from my heart...what I'm 'posed' to play."

Late nights, after he's completed his chef's turn at the Hunter House, Espy sits in with bands at Tybee bars until the early morning hours, drawing high praise from both musicians and customers.

He came by his musical and artistic side honestly since his mother was an accomplished pianist who also delved deeply into the arts.

"She had me playing the piano when I was a kid," he says. "She always said, you know, if you can play a piano, you can play anything, but that formal stuff wasn't for me."

Espy says his dad had little appreciation for either classical music or the various areas of art in which his mother was involved.

He was a barnstorming pilot in the early days of aviation and flew with Gen. Claire Chennault's Flying Tigers in China during World War II when he was shot down twice and captured by the Japanese.

"Dad's idea of music was the Army Air Corps song, but he did have a great talent for making money," says Espy, noting that his father retired at age 37 and now lives in Beaufort.

Espy's parents divorced when he was a teenager, and he attended high schools in Savannah, Atlanta, and Tampa, Florida while living intermittently with one parent or the other.

"We had a pretty wide-open relationship, and they let me do pretty much what I wanted to as long as I didn't get in a lot of trouble," he says.

Espy did get into a bit of stickiness in connection with LSD at age 20, when he dropped a little and passed a bit after spending a year at Carnegie Mellon College in Pittsburgh, Pennsylvania.

"I was just doing it for fun and adventure, wanting to be like Timothy Leary and spread it around a little," he explains, noting that he "got lucky" when he got off, indicted, but untried and unincarcerated, after scrutiny by the FBI.

Chastened, he returned south to attend the Atlanta College of Art, which he recalls as "a great place, a wide-open school. They had great teachers, but after a while I felt that it was a little too rigid and just went off on my own."

Espy was successful with art shows and exhibits in the

Atlanta area while making frequent trips down to Myrtle Beach in an old VW van. While hanging out at the beach he produced dozens of realistic watercolors, then took them back to Atlanta where they sold "in bunches. I was doing real well."

Despite his relative success, after a couple of years he decided it was time to get more serious about his painting and wrote postcards to famous artists he admired, offering to serve as an apprentice to develop his talent.

Two of those he contacted, Santo Bruno, an Italian painter who had taught at Temple University, and Kinje Akagawa, an internationally known Japanese print maker and sumi-e (watercolor brush painting) artist, responded.

Both painters wound up teaching at the Atlanta College of Art and assisted Espy in getting a scholarship to return to the school while he worked with them.

Espy ultimately graduated, then got a master's degree from Georgia State University.

In addition to staging shows in New York, he spent the next seven years working and doing shows with Kinje, who impressed him instantly when he attended his first design course in Atlanta.

"All the students came in with all this art material - India ink, pens, paper, brushes, and stuff - and Akagawa waved a piece of newsprint in front of the class and said the first week's assignment was to make the paper as black as possible, anyway we wanted."

"Students came to the next class with all sorts of examples, soaking their paper in ink, that sort of thing."

After examining them all, "Kinje struck a match and burned his newsprint showing us the most simplistic way to create pure black from the material. It blew us away."

The next assignment was to turn a piece of newsprint from one dimensional to three dimensional and students returned the next week with dozens of elaborate three dimensional exhibits.

Kinje simply burned a sheet of newsprint again.

"It went from a flat sheet to a ball of carbon. That was what he was about, turning the complex into the simple. He was into a technique called 'flammage'... burning things. He was a child in Hiroshima (when the atomic bomb dropped), and it affected his entire life and art."

After obtaining his master's degree, Espy opened a large art studio in Atlanta where he employed a number of artists and started working non-stop for hours at a time.

"Man, there'd be days of old meals which had been brought in and beer cans lying all over the place," he chuckles.

As his reputation grew, he started dividing his activities between his Atlanta studio and his shows in New York.

By this time, Espy says his art had changed dramatically, from representational watercolors to a highly conceptual, intensely personal form of art he called

Espy Geissler reflects on music and cooking.

"music at the speed of light."

"I always liked music better than anything, and I liked painting more than playing an instrument. I developed this thing of taking all the elements of music and how to interpret them visually in paint. The results are simple and yet very abstract impressionistic."

Despite their seeming simplicity, however, the designs are carefully thought out. The concept is that a painting is much like a piece of music, he says.

"You follow a musical score much like you read a book (from top to bottom, left to right). In a painting what happens is you see it all at once. You don't read it like a book. It's all happening immediately. It's like if you took a Chopin sonata which had 4,320 different notes in it and you had that many pianos and players and they all hit that many notes at the same time. It would be up to your ears to define a melody in there.

"When one looks at an abstract painting it's much the same thing except the impact is all at the one time. Work on the painting happens over a period of time, but the viewing of it is immediate.

"What I've had to do in my art is to develop keys that will lead you through a story. Once you've found a key in one of these paintings you start seeing another perspective, a different image proportion, and all of a sudden what looked like it was flat, like a surface that someone took sticks with fur on the end and smushed colored liquids around on, becomes an intensely graphic, vibrant field of color and richness and time.

"You can actually spend time looking at these things and feel like you've been somewhere visually. It will come to you."

When a casual viewer of his work asks Espy to explain what a specific painting means, he responds enigmatically: "I can't explain it to you. It is the explanation."

While in New York for one of his shows he met Titou Quiquerez, an Algerian Frenchman who owned Chez Jacqueline, a small, exclusive French-Mediterranean style restaurant near Greenwich Village.

"You had to have a reservation six months in advance to get into his place," according to Espy.

Titou took him under his wing, teaching him about exotic food preparation, introducing him to obscure but excellent restaurants in New York, and generally "educating my palette," says Espy. "He gave me a real feel for food and food preparation."

Titou also spent time with Espy in Atlanta, where they opened a food catering service for exclusive parties.

Although his art studio and catering service continued to do well, Espy got antsy after a while and decided he was ready to return to Tybee and the beach he had enjoyed so much as a youth.

"I just walked in the studio and said 'I'm outta here', he says, chuckling as he recalls that "they figured I'd just had a bad lunch and asked me what I was going to do at Tybee, wherever that was. I said: Hell, I don't know. I'm just going back where I came from."

And he did.

That was about seven years ago.

Initially, though living on the island, Espy worked for an artist magazine that specialized in air brush art, and he toured the country conducting seminars featuring this art form.

That ended after his son was seriously injured when he was hit by a car just after stepping off his school bus, causing Espy to sink into severe depression.

Unable to work, he started hanging around on the porch of the Hunter House, drinking martinis and "complaining about the food."

The owner, John Hunter, became exasperated after a while and asked Espy if he thought he could do any better.

"I said, yeah, I thought so, and invited him over to my house for dinner the next week," recalls Espy.

Hunter liked the food, came over several more times, and when his regular chef went on vacation, he invited Espy to cook in his restaurant.

It wasn't long before Espy became the regular chef and the restaurant's business started booming.

The average number of weekend diners has grown from about a dozen a night to 70 or more, and the menu has evolved from plain American fare to eclectic offerings Espy describes as a "fusion type of cuisine" including Japanese garnishing and "renderings from Spanish preparations which are picturesque and labor intensive."

Espy says one of his signature dishes "is seafood carbonara with shrimp, scallops, and crab sauteed with prosciutto, cheese, and mushrooms. Added to that is an asiago-based alfredo sauce poured over black and white fettuccine, served with gingered carrots. It's a very visual meal."

The cuisine caught on, with repeat customers making reservations days in advance and a number of rave reviews being printed in the Atlanta newspapers and the New York Times.

Along the way, when Hunter's silent partner wanted out, he offered Espy the chance to become co-owner, and Espy quickly bought in.

Visitors and residents alike have been buying into Espy's cooking, art, and musicianship ever since.

POSTSCRIPT: The Hunter House was sold several years after this was written, and Espy retired. He and his wife are now living quietly near Horsepen Creek.

Debbie Brady Robinson -

She Painted Her Way to Paradise

Banker

Stockbroker

Lives for Art

One of the area's most successful artists learned her trade on Tybee, then returned to practice it after a stellar career elsewhere in high finance.

Debbie Brady Robinson, whose sweet nature is reflected in her charmingly realistic canvasses, claims she has found happiness on the beach she cavorted about as a child.

"That's what Tybee is to me," she says. "It's paradise."

But while her roots in both art and the island were planted early, her journey to their rediscovery was not as easy as the feather light strokes of her brush.

Debbie, who radiates the iridescent nature of those who genuinely care, springs from a family laden with artistic talent.

"I grew up with art all around me," she says.

Her father, Jack Brady, a real estate broker who brought the family to Savannah from New Orleans when Debbie was six months old, painted and sketched much of his life.

He painted the walls of his daughter's room with fairy tale characters and created a canopy of an evening sky on the ceiling, sprinkling it with stars and constellations she could gaze upon as she fell asleep to dream of producing similar scenes from her own palette.

A great aunt, Mary Lucille Brady, was an accomplished portrait artist in Savannah, and an aunt, Corrine Brady Owen, and cousin, Beth Anderson Toth, are artists on Tybee.

Cumulatively, they passed their passion for painting along to Debbie when she was still a tot.

"I never wanted to do or be anything but an artist," she says, flashing her invariably infectious smile while radiating the aura of someone who genuinely cares about both her craft and humanity in general.

Debbie started early, drawing on scraps of paper in her preschool days when other girls were playing with dolls, and pursuing her penchant for painting when she started school at St. Michael's after her family moved to Tybee in 1963.

Island artist Yon Swanson offered instruction for grammar school students at St. Michael's and, "I just loved those art lessons," she says.

"It's funny, but I've talked with former schoolmates in recent years, and they don't even remember the lessons."

The lessons made such an indelible impression on Debbie that she now returns to the school once a week to instruct students, because "I want to give something back to the place that gave me so much."

After completing the eighth grade at St. Michael's in 1972, Debbie continued honing her artistic skills in high school at St. Vincent's and Savannah High, the

Debbie Brady Robinson reflects on art.

latter being her first exposure to a public school.

Debbie confesses she transferred to Savannah High after her sophomore year because of her puppy love attraction to a male student there.

While she thrived on her newfound social exposure in public school, she says the education it provided was considerably below St. Vincent's standards.

When she attended her first English session at Savannah High, Debbie says she was convinced they had mistakenly assigned her to a remedial class.

She later learned the class was really for advanced students and wound up skipping a year in school.

"I didn't get a lot of academic education there, but I did get a good education in life," she smiles, noting that by the time of her early graduation, the young love which prompted her transfer had long since gone by the boards.

Debbie painted the pictures which adorned the covers of school yearbooks and other publications for both of the high schools she attended, while producing hundreds of drawings and paintings in her spare time.

Most of her early work was tucked in a large trunk stored away in an attic. Unfortunately, the trunk was misplaced somewhere along the way.

"Nobody has seen it for years," she says.

Debbie credits Sally Bostwick, a celebrated Tybee artist for more than 40 years, with stoking the flames of her own artistic zeal.

"It was her art that I saw around the island as a child," says Debbie. "I loved her work. You can look at one of her paintings and know it's Little Tybee. You just know the place. My attempts to capture the beauty of the island with my painting were inspired by her art."

Debbie fulfilled her desire to meet her idol only recently, when one of her art students turned out to be Sally's grandson. She had the boy take a note to his grandmother saying she wanted to meet her and purchase one of her paintings.

They finally got together at an art show last July. Debbie left the show with not only a new friend and fellow admirer but a long-coveted painting by Sally, much of whose recent work is now on display at the Tybee Arts Association's new Lighthouse Art Gallery on Butler Avenue.

Sally has just been named the association's Artist of the Month for March.

Debbie was instrumental in setting up the new gallery, which recently moved from its former site beside the Tybee Lighthouse. She is currently the association's vice president in charge of the gallery.

After high school Debbie moved on to Georgia Southern University where she majored in art.

After her sophomore year she took a divergent path which led her business career.

That summer she returned to her New Orleans birthplace and spent a lot of time witnessing and working with that city's art community, members of which converge daily on the city's Jackson Square.

Debbie discusses art with customer at gallery.

"Many of them were excellent artists, ten times better than I was at the time," says the self-effacing Debbie. "It was so sad seeing them. They were almost starving and many of them were older people. I just couldn't see myself doing that. I knew I didn't want to be a starving artist."

Disenchanted and determined to avoid such a fate, Debbie hastily changed her major to journalism and then business when she returned to Georgia Southern, a decision which dramatically altered the course of her next 13 years.

Upon graduation, she was employed by the Great Southern Federal Bank, which later became First Federal Savings and Loan.

She started as a loan servicing representative, then moved up quickly to the positions of teller, new accounts rep, savings specialist, assistant branch manager, branch manager, assistant vice president and vice president.

In 1977, she was lured to Brunswick to help operate a branch bank for Savannah First Federal. First Georgia Bank later purchased the branch but kept Debbie on as its manager and later vice president of operations.

Now noted for her financial acumen, she was recruited to work with a Frederica Bank and Trust start-up bank on St. Simon's Island, where she was placed in charge of everything but lending.

Motivated by financial success, Debbie decided the quickest route to riches was self-employment, so she became a stockbroker in Brunswick.

She rapidly built a list of 300 clients but soon learned there was a downside to such success.

"I had thought there was a lot of stress in banking - most bankers do - but try being a stockbroker and see what happens," she laughs. "I was working all the time, seven days a week, many times as late as 1:00 a.m., then took calls at my home at all hours of the night.

"I tried to handle every client as if they were my only one. Nobody had to worry about their money because I worried about it all the time. It killed me to see anybody lose any money."

While extremely successful, she was unhappy, and the stressful work wreaked havoc on her health.

After five years as a stockbroker, the work was literally killing her.

Debbie was hospitalized with off-the-scale high blood pressure. Doctors discovered that while in the hospital, where she was repeatedly, her blood pressure would drop to normal, then skyrocket again when she returned to work.

"It got to the point where I could feel it (the rise in blood pressure) coming on, which is unusual," she says.

Her doctor urged her to change her life, warning that if she continued in her occupation, she could count on being dead within a year.

That warning, rendered in 1995, made an indelible impression on the financial wizard.

"I was devastated," she recalls. "I didn't know what to do, and my clients kept calling me at home at all hours."

In desperation, Debbie took a break to head for her parents' Tybee beach house to get her priorities in order.

"When I walked on the beach, I knew this was my place," she recalls. "This was my paradise! I didn't want to be anywhere else."

Debbie's health and attitude improved, and she shared this revelation with her husband, Mark, an industrial parts salesman who worked out of their home in Brunswick.

Mark concurred with his wife, took another job in industrial sales with a firm which needed a representative in the Savannah area, and joined Debbie on Tybee where she blossomed by becoming immersed in her lifelong love of art.

Debbie is a prolific producer, sometimes working on four or five projects simultaneously, mostly painting in the wee morning hours between midnight and 4:00 a.m.

"That's the time when the phone doesn't ring, and nobody's looking over your shoulder," she smiles. "Besides, I learned long ago that it was useless for me to try to sleep when a painting was on my mind."

Once back in stride, Debbie joined the Tybee Arts Association and was delighted to discover her work sold well.

Debbie displays some of her art.

"It's been a real surprise," she says. "I took a left turn, but now I'm back doing the only thing I ever wanted to do. And I'm not starving! I couldn't be happier. And it takes a lot less money to live on Tybee than it does other places."

Working from her imagination, Debbie's paintings resonate with realism, and she has no fear of running out of ideas.

"I'll never be able to paint everything that I want to paint," she says. "There are so many things I want to paint that if I had two lifetimes, I couldn't do it all."

She has limited edition lithograph prints made from her most popular paintings for sale to those who can't afford her originals but are anxious to acquire her work.

Prints of her paintings of the island's new Pavilion and a montage of scenes from the popular book *Midnight in the Garden of Good and Evil* have been her sales leaders.

She has sold dozens of her prints to raise funds for the renovation of the Tybee Lighthouse, and she gets frequent requests to remarque prints, painting original images of those who purchase them on the reproduction.

While Debbie does excellent work in oil and watercolors, acrylics are her principal medium because she prefers to paint rapidly and says working with oil is too slow.

Her artwork is now displayed in shops throughout the area and into South Florida as far as Venice and Sarasota, where she has recently been requested to put on a one-woman show.

She's also semi-back in business as manager of the new Lighthouse Art Gallery, though she expects to spend less time there once it is firmly established.

"But I'll always be there on the weekends," she says. "Those are the busiest times."

Her husband has just joined her to make art a family occupation.

Mark, who started framing his wife's artwork some time ago, became an outstanding craftsman as he grew enamored of the work.

"He's great at it," says Debbie. "He's so meticulous."

Fellow artists concurred, and Mark got so many requests to do their framing he has opened his own business, "The Hall of Frames," in a room off the main display area in the gallery.

Debbie displays her art and Mark's frames in gallery.

"We both love the work and the island, and I just want to keep on doing what I do forever," says Debbie. "I couldn't be happier."

Who wouldn't be after finding their personal paradise?

POSTSCRIPT: Debbie has gained a reputation as one of the most popular and talented artists in the area. She and Mark opened the "Hall of Frames and Debbie Brady Robinson Signature Gallery" beside Highway 80, where they displayed their work for years. They sold the studio in 2016 to go "off on an adventure for a while," according to Debbie.

Ed Towns -

A Disappearing Breed of Hero

Cohesion Beneath The Sea

On the surface, he's been extraordinarily successful.

He established the first nursing home on Tybee Island, served two terms on the island's city council and acquired and subdivided one of the largest, most secluded, and valuable pieces of property on the island.

But the thing that had the biggest impact on his life is not on the surface at all. It's beneath it, where only a handful of hearty souls have ventured, and once having done so, found themselves inextricably bound to one another by the experience.

Ed Towns was a World War II submariner and says not a day goes by that he doesn't recall some aspects, ranging from harrowing to hilarious, of that service.

"I don't know what it is about submarine duty," he says. "You're just drawn to it like some magnetic force. I can't describe it, but once serving aboard a sub in the war you just had to do it, not to prove anything, and not because you weren't afraid, because we were all afraid, but you couldn't resist it."

"There's a cohesion, a camaraderie, among submariners that you don't find anyplace else. I guess we had to be close."

Most of those brave seaman from the big war have maintained their ties throughout the years, frequently attending meetings together and visiting submarine bases to inspect the new underwater craft, but their number is declining rapidly.

"There are only about 3,000 of us left, and they're dying off fast," says Ed. "A lot of us go down to Kings Bay quite often. The commandant there is good to us old veterans."

Ed, a member of Georgia's Sealion (named for the submarine Sealion, the first U.S. sub sunk in the war off Manila) Chapter of U.S. Submarine Veterans of World

Ed 'Cuz' Towns discusses change in submarines

War II, recently made a five-day voyage aboard the Tennessee, one of the Navy's newest nuclear submarines.

He says there's a big difference between the new subs and the "fleet boats" on which he served, particularly in size.

The modern subs are over 640 feet long compared with just over 300 for the old ones, and the crew size now runs about 150, twice as many as those on the old ones.

The new subs have areas adjacent to their missile silos big enough to jog around and roomy circular stairways, according to Ed, who says:

"The funny thing is they don't seem to have as much room per person as we did. They have a lot more hot bunks (shared bunks where one seaman sleeps while the other is on duty) than we used to have."

Ed has a special submarine veteran license plate on his car and is frequently stopped by other sub veterans who want to discuss shared experiences.

He is originally from Dublin, Georgia, well not really Dublin, but a little place near it on the Oconee River in Laurens County.

Ed says its proper name is "Daughnaughclaughnaughbaugh," an old Indian name, but folks around there shortened it to "Barneyclabber" for understandable reasons.

His father was a true entrepreneur.

He had a farm, a timber and cotton gin business, a

paddlewheel boat for hauling cotton, a barrel stave manufacturing mill, and other enterprises in the Dublin area, but, like many businessmen, he was wiped out when the stock market crashed.

"Everything went to pot," says Ed. "My father lost everything but the farm, and three wealthy businessmen in Dublin committed suicide. A banker jumped off a seven-story building, the highest one in town. Another man shot himself with a .38 in his back yard, and a third cut his throat in his bathtub."

"My father came home and told us we were broke, but he said, 'I'm not going to commit suicide'."

The family survived with food from their farm, while bartering for other necessities.

"Folks kind of looked out for each other back then," says Ed.

Eventually, his father got work surveying timber for big insurance companies that were buying up land, and in 1936, just out of high school, Ed took a job with Union Bag in Savannah and started sowing a field full of wild oats.

He had two buddies, who, like Ed, made $30 a week at what he still calls "The Bag," and they pooled their funds to rent a furnished apartment on Tybee for $45 a month.

"We were a trio of party guys," laughs Ed.

They had some pretty wild weekends at the apartment and you can bet that it was Ed, an unrepentant ladies' man at the time, who was the leader of the pack.

"We'd go up to the pier and dance all night to the big bands," he recalls. "We just had a ball!"

Ed had a date with a school teacher one night when Bob Crosby was playing on the pier, but it didn't turn out the way he planned.

He says he had "a little too much to drink" and decided to take a swim, but "that was a big mistake."

"I got caught in an undertow, and the last thing I could get to was a pier piling. I wrapped myself around it, and by the time I got out, I was cut up all over from the barnacles. I was a mess!"

His buddies hauled him back to their pad where they patched up his wounds, but that pretty much ended his amorous plans for the evening.

He was back in stride before long, however, getting hooked up with an attractive young woman from Fort Screven who, unbeknownst to Ed, was the wife of a serviceman at the fort.

"They were getting a divorce, but he didn't like my fooling around with his wife," he laughs. "He came after me with a gun one day. That's when I checked out of The Bag and said it's time to get in the Navy."

Ed went through boot camp and then to radio school in Charleston.

Pearl Harbor was bombed the day before he graduated.

Ed says he didn't jump into the submarine service because of some innate love of the craft. He was "volunteered" after first serving on the battleships Wyoming and Arkansas, which sailed to Britain during the bombing there.

"I met a lot of girls in Edinburgh and Paisley during a week layover," he laughs. "We were in the right spot, and you know how Navy boys are."

The Arkansas hit heavy winds and high seas in the North Atlantic on his last trip from England, wallowing and pitching so steeply that its screws cleared the water.

Ed says most of those aboard got seasick when saltwater contaminated the ship's fresh water supply.

The USS Wakefield, a luxury liner which had been converted to a troop ship and was part of the convoy, burned during the crossing.

Ed considers one of the worst parts of the voyage was when his crew was not allowed to debark in New York because their ship had to be fumigated for lice.

"Here we were at the best port in the world, looking for a party, and we can't go ashore," he laments.

Just after anchoring, the Arkansas communications officer got word that men were needed for submarine duty, but no one volunteered.

"So he put three names in a hat and pulled them out, and I was picked," says 'Cuz,' as he was dubbed by his new submariner comrades.

He was quickly sent to sub school in Connecticut for four months and says that although he had to be pushed into the service, it turned out to be the best break of his life.

Cuz soon learned there were numerous perks, called "slack," associated with being a submariner, and they started almost immediately.

Sailors were allowed to have two beers with their lunch during sub school, though this was really a calculated gratuity since testing occurred immediately after lunch, and he figured the Navy wanted to see how the recruits handled their liquor to determine if any had a drinking problem.

Ed displays model of his old submarine.

He discovered other “slack” benefits were even better after winning his dolphins, the submariner insignia granted after training and a couple of wartime cruises were completed to make sure new men are really cut out for submarine duty.

Cuz says he was hooked on subs after his first dive, and those slack benefits were just the icing on his cake.

In addition to the food being excellent, submariners were permitted to ramble around Honolulu all night while those in other units had an 11:30 p.m. curfew. The sub crews stayed in the Royal Hawaiian Hotel when they returned to Pearl Harbor from patrols, and Cuz and his buddies cut a wicked swath through the city.

Sometimes sub skippers would get in fights in the BOQ after patrols when they'd had a few drinks and started arguing about whose boat had sunk the most ships.

“They'd just tear the place up,” says Cuz.

He also remembers a fight between his crew and that of the submarine Trigger following a big poker game in “The Pink Lady,” as they called the Royal Hawaiian.

“It just erupted,” he says. “It was boat against boat, and we were into it all up and down the hall. One of my buddies hit me by mistake and knocked me all the way down a flight of stairs.”

Cuz says he halted the melee by grabbing a fire extinguisher off a wall and spraying the entire area.

Another special perk was that enlisted men on sub duty were not required to salute officers routinely and there was no "spit and polish" dress code while they were aboard their ship.

The crews were permitted to smoke pretty much when they wanted and were "officially" given alcohol on occasion.

The submariners also received 55 percent more than the regular pay for their ranks, which was five percent more than even the carrier-based sailors received.

"That last five percent was called 'dungaree' pay, since we were exposed to diesel fumes all the time, and they figured it cost us more to wash our clothes," laughs Cuz. "The carrier boys didn't like that."

Clearly, Cuz had found his niche, but just as clearly there was a serious downside.

Fifty-two of the 300 subs in service during World War II were sunk, and the odds got worse with the number of patrols.

Early in the war there were the frustrations that came when U.S. subs venturing into harm's way took dead aim at ships in enemy convoys, fired their torpedoes and made direct hits only to find the torpedoes failed to detonate.

"We saw some of them hit ships broadside and broach, coming up out of the water on the side of the ship and falling back without exploding," says Cuz.

Those failed torpedoes sometimes led to attacks on subs which had nothing to show for the danger they faced.

Those were the worst of times, he says.

The problem was mostly eliminated later in the war with improved firing pins, "and that's when we really started to sink some ships out there, mostly in '43 and '44," he says.

Improvements were also made to propulsion systems when the Americans were able to copy components of German torpedoes and eliminate the telltale smoke from their own alcohol propelled torpedoes.

The Haddock (SS-231), to which Cuz was assigned for most of the war, carried both alcohol and electric powered torpedoes. The former were a lot faster but left a wake which was easy to detect. The electric ones ran deep and left no wake but were about 20 knots slower through the water.

Depth-charge attacks were especially harrowing for submariners who had to helplessly hunker down beneath the sea with charges exploding all around.

The trauma caused by those explosions was more than some could stand, according to Cuz, who remembers one crewmate who broke down during an attack and had to be strapped in a straitjacket.

The submarines were rigged to run silent during such attacks, but Japanese ships got better and better at attacking them as the war proceeded, he says.

"They learned to drop depth charges deep, getting below our subs, and you were pretty much a goner if they exploded close under you."

After eight hours or so below the surface, the air turned

bad and crewmen were bathed in perspiration and stress, as they were forced to creep around in special slippers to maintain complete silence.

If someone dropped something on the deck, he was immediately admonished by shipmates, since any noise could reveal their position to ships above.

Ed says special CO2 absorbent was dispensed and spread on bed coverings to eliminate some of the crew's exhaled carbon dioxide, and although "it didn't give us any more oxygen, but it helped clear the air."

Some sailors developed premonitions about impending disaster after a few patrols and opted out of the service.

One of Cuz's buddies did that, saying he just felt it was time to get out when they returned to Pearl Harbor for a three-week leave.

He says his buddy refused to take the leave, feeling he didn't deserve it, and instead signed on to the submarine *Seawolf* for one more run.

The *Seawolf* was sunk on that patrol.

Far too frequently, Cuz and his shipmates got word that submarines were overdue.

"They weren't reported overdue until they were 10 days or so late, and it was almost certain that they were lost when those reports came in," he says.

Cuz lost a lot of friends in the war.

One special problem about service in the Pacific was that the water was so clear a sub's silhouette could be spotted by planes even when it was running relatively deep.

There was one advantage to the area, however. Subs were sometimes able to find a "thermal gradient" at a depth of about 250 feet where they could kill all engines and float in eerie, almost undetectable silence.

Not only did the density of the gradient allow them to linger there without power, but it also deflected signals from Japanese sonar, scattering sound and making them hard to spot.

Cuz smiles as he recalls adventures at sea.

"We'd dive to about 300 feet and then ease back up and you'd feel the ship slow a little," says Cuz. "When the thermograph needle was at 45 degrees, you knew you were there. It was a layer of colder water over warmer water or warm over cold. The captain loved it when we were able to hit that spot."

Cuz says submariners are "special people" who are somehow "different."

"We took pride in ourselves and our shipmates," he says. "That's what kept us coming back. It wasn't just patriotism. It was kind of a mystic attraction."

He takes justifiable pride in the fact that, while the service made up only one percent of total Navy forces, it sunk 55 percent of all Japanese ship tonnage.

Most subs went out alone, rarely forming wolfpacks like the Germans did. And with a range of 13,000 miles, they covered enormous distances on their solo voyages.

Cuz was assigned to communications in the radio shack of the Haddock, which sank 26 Japanese ships and received the Presidential Unit Citation for extraordinary heroism in action against an armed enemy, the equivalent of a Medal of Honor for a ship.

Even amid all the trauma, however, Cuz remembers some rollicking good times.

Returning from shore leave where he learned the art of distilling liquor, he set up a small still in a corner of the radio shack and started a batch using raisins and pineapple, covering his concoction with cheese cloth while it fermented.

It was a distinctly furtive operation, given the fact that his skipper was a teetotaling Christian Scientist.

Unfortunately, Cuz was studiously concentrating on something else when his brew hit the height of fermentation and exploded, splattering him and his equipment with raisins.

A lieutenant came by at that precise moment demanding to know what was going on.

After Cuz sheepishly confessed, the officer asked for a taste. They downed one together "and it was pretty good," he recalls.

Better than the booze was the fact that no one was the wiser once he cleaned the area and the odor dissipated.

Home brew was not the only alcohol the crew had access to, however. Their alcohol powered torpedoes provided a popular beverage called "gili" for many of the crewmen.

"A lot of the officers drank gili, too," says Cuz. "It tasted pretty good, but you couldn't drink much of it. That was pure alcohol. Ran about 300 proof! Grapefruit juice or coffee worked good with it, and you didn't get much of a hangover."

Small portions of gili were generally passed out to the men after intensive depth charge attacks, even when the sub was under the command of the abstinent captain.

Cuz, being Cuz, devised means for more frequent access

to the gili, of course.

"It's always good to know the pharmacist mate," he smiles wryly. "We were good buddies, and he didn't take a very good inventory."

He also recalls the time he went ashore on Guam, where the U.S. had cleared an encampment while Japanese troops still roamed nearby and "one day we caught a Jap in the mess hall."

Cuz and a buddy convinced a pilot to fly in some real liquor, paying him $50 a fifth.

They shared most of it with their buddies but kept one bottle and spread out on the sand to enjoy it, sipping a bit, then napping and sipping again, while hiding their treasure in the sand with only its neck protruding.

After one of those naps, however, they awakened to find the bottle was missing.

Both became furious, but his buddy was really stomping mad.

He scaled a tall coconut palm beside the metal Quonset hut where the rest of their shipmates were sleeping and started bombarding it with coconuts.

"Scared the hell out of them," laughs Cuz. "They thought they were under attack. When they finally settled down, he'd do it again, lying flat up in that tree where no one could spot him. It was hilarious!"

Like every sailor, Cuz learned that it's the enlisted men, not the officers, who are really in charge of their ships.

When the Haddock took on a new CO after its regular captain was injured in an accident off Guam, they quickly learned that he was a real gung-ho type with very little battle experience.

"I could feel there was dissension aboard, even among the officers," says Cuz.

"We got into a couple of Japanese convoys and didn't get anything but one or two damaged ships and got the hell beat out of us with depth charges. The crew didn't like him much."

Their disdain for the new captain was exacerbated when he announced he was changing the standard practice of diving for safety when an aircraft was within 2,000 yards of the sub, saying he wanted to see how close a plane could get and still give him time to dive.

The new captain said he wouldn't dive until an aircraft was 1,000 yards away.

From a long distance "most of the planes couldn't tell whether we were friend or foe but they could easily see your silhouette if you weren't deep enough when they flew over," says Cuz. "The guys were really worried."

He and a buddy remedied the problem before it led to disaster. They re-calibrated the ship's radar so that when an aircraft was 2,000 yards away, it reflected 1,000 yards, and the captain never found out.

Cuz had completed seven patrols aboard the Haddock, each ranging from 40 to 60 days, by the time the war was winding down.

He was overdue for rotation back to the U.S., since most seaman rotated after five or six patrols, and was elated when informed it was now his turn.

Then he got the bad news. They needed a replacement chief for the submarine Cero (SS-225) because theirs had been bitten by a barracuda while swimming off Saipan. Cuz says barracuda abounded in those waters, and Seabees had to build wire barricades around swimming areas to keep them out, but one apparently got in and attacked the chief.

Cuz, who was now a chief, was the man they said they wanted.

He says he dipped into the gili pretty good before undergoing the psychiatric evaluation all submariners were required to take intermittently to ensure they were still fully fit, but despite his dubious state, he was cleared for the new assignment with no trouble.

"I could tell the psychiatrist had sipped a few drinks too," Cuz laughs.

He was disappointed his return to the U.S. was delayed, but that wasn't the worst of it.

He very nearly didn't make it back at all, while learning first hand that planes can mistake friends for foes.

The Cero was cruising on the surface through the Kuril Straits near Japan in a fog, figuring there was little danger since the war was almost over and few Japanese planes or ships would be in the area.

That's when a plane spotted them and dropped a wing bomb before the lookout could sound a warning.

"It really got us," recalls Cuz. "It bent our periscopes,

and we were shipping water and just barely got under. A lot of us believe it was a friendly plane."

Cuz was hit on the head by a falling insulator, and there was confusion aboard since the sub was in darkness, having lost all its power.

"We knew we had to surface because of the damage and the water we were taking on, and the periscopes were useless," he says. "We had to go up blind."

The captain told Cuz they were heading topside and ordered him to get a distress message out "quick," calling for air cover since he assumed, if the attacking plane was Japanese, it would call for others to search for their crippled vessel.

Cuz says he figured the main antennae had been destroyed by the bomb, and when they surfaced to check, "it was in the drink like I thought."

It became his job to rig a makeshift emergency antenna, without which no distress call could be made.

"They strapped life vests and lines to me, and I crawled, slipping and sliding all the way, out to the bull nose (the large hole on the bow of the sub through which its anchor chain is fed) and hooked up one end of the antenna cable," says Cuz, shivering slightly with the memory. "That water was freezing out there."

Then he says he crawled back and attached the other end of the cable to the sub's A frame before going back below to make the distress call to Pearl Harbor in such a rush that "I don't think we even encrypted it."

The call went through, and several allied planes arrived

Ed wears vest displaying ribbons earned during his submarine service.

as air cover, rotating with others as the Cero limped toward Midway. The trip took five days.

Following repairs, they headed for Pearl Harbor.

During the voyage, Cuz approached his captain to tell him he was scheduled for rotation and wanted to be the first man off the ship when they arrived.

"I'm going to give you that privilege," the CO replied. "You deserve it! I was standing there waiting by the gangplank when we got in, and I was the first man off. Everybody laughed about it."

The Japanese surrendered just after his arrival, and Cuz was discharged in November of 1945 after serving from the beginning to the end of the war.

After his discharge, he returned to Dublin, and to his peacetime name of Ed.

It was there that he met and married his wife, Jewell, a Navy nurse who was working at the Dublin hospital.

"She outranked me," he laughs. "She was a lieutenant, and we got married when she was on leave. Then she put in for her discharge."

Ed worked for four years with metal X-rays using first radium and then cobalt 60 inspecting welds on large storage tanks in Augusta for DuPont.

Then he purchased a drive-in barbecue restaurant and a drugstore in Dublin, "but I couldn't make any money at it" so he moved to Jacksonville, where he worked as an assistant manager for a Western Auto store.

All the while, Ed remained in the Navy Reserves, going

on inactive status because of his frequent employment moves.

He was called up when they needed experienced submariners during the Korean "Conflict."

"There were only six of us in Duval County who were qualified submariners from World War II, and we were all called up," he says.

It turned out to be like old home week because his old ship, the Haddock, was berthed on the St. Johns River in Jacksonville at the time.

Cuz says the duty was pretty good because he was stationed in Key West aboard the Trumpetfish (SS-425), mostly cruising around the Caribbean on training missions.

The bad part was that they were testing a new snorkel device to permit subs to run deeper underwater while operating on diesel power rather than batteries.

Ed says the snorkels wreaked havoc with his ears due to the changing air pressure created by the device, and when he was offered a land-based job communicating with submarines on training missions in Norfolk, Virginia he took the position, remaining there until the Korean Conflict was resolved.

After that, he sold hospital supplies in Georgia and Alabama for a couple of years, while his wife was employed as head of a nursing home.

It was through his sales job that he discovered the old Army hospital at Fort Screven on Tybee was on the market.

Jewell was enthusiastic about the possibility of operating her own nursing home, and it was for her that Ed bought the former hospital in 1956, turning it into one of the first nursing homes in Georgia.

Jewell ran the nursing home, starting off with just three or four patients, while Ed worked in Savannah.

"When I got the place, people said I was crazy, that nobody would want to go all the way out to Tybee to a nursing home," he laughs. "It turned out that people loved to be at the beach, and we did quite well."

Once business picked up, he demolished the old hospital building and constructed a new 50-bed nursing home in its place.

They operated the establishment until 1980, at which time they sold it and retired.

Meanwhile, Ed also did well with other real estate ventures on Tybee.

He purchased 39 acres at what is now called Eagles Nest in the mid-1970s, building a house at the south end of the property featuring expansive views of the marsh and creek.

His attractive home is situated on one of the most secluded spots on Tybee with a half-mile of woods between it and the nearest house.

Ed used to keep horses, goats, and pigs on the property, but he got rid of them.

The goats posed the biggest problem with their proliferation. He started with a dozen, and when their num-

Ed looks over the marsh behind his Eagles Nest home. The names of the submarines on which he served are listed on the back of his vest

ber increased to 25, they were getting out of hand.

"I gave them all away to a man on the promise that he would come out and round 'em up and haul 'em away," he laughs.

Over the years, Ed has sold just over half of his original holdings, that portion fronting U.S. 80 which is furthest away from his secluded home. Some of the island's most prestigious houses are now located on that property.

Jewell passed away in 1991, just a year after their son died of cancer, and Ed recently purchased a condominium where he plans to move after selling his house.

"This place is just too big for me now," he says.

Meanwhile, he's doing a bit of fishing on two freshwater ponds he built near his house.

And between trips to Kings Bay and other submarine bases to meet with his buddies, he spends a lot of time with his model submarine collection and other memorabilia connected with his submariner's life that are spread throughout his house.

"There's not a day goes by that I don't think about some phase of submarine duty," he says. "It'll never leave me."

Those were the glory days for Cuz and the brave comrades who shared them with him.

POSTSCRIPT: Edward Willard Towns moved into that condo before he passed away on Nov. 22, 2002, at age 84. His picturesque old house is no longer secluded. Virtually all the land leading up to it is now occupied by dozens of upscale houses. A goat might have trouble finding a spot to graze in that area now.

Jodee Sadowsky -

"World Famous" Lives Up to Name

Island Chef Drawing A Crowd

He's the Big Kahuna of tomorrow's 13th annual Beach Bum Parade and of the most famous breakfast emporium on Tybee every day in the year.

Joseph "Jodee" Sadowsky, proprietor of the World Famous Breakfast Club where the elite, and virtually everybody else, meet to eat their first meal of the day, is acknowledged as Tybee's egg-flipping king.

His breakfasts are embellished in more ways than a belly dancer moves, and customers stand patiently in lines stretching down the block patiently waiting for a seat in his restaurant.

"It's crazy," he says, observing clientele standing in pouring rain or blazing sunshine while nearby restaurants have space to spare and could serve them immediately.

Early mornings, or in the off season, the restaurant is a gathering place for local residents who sit at the counter exchanging jokes and catching up on the latest gossip on an island where gossip easily edges out TV and newspapers as the favored form of entertainment and enlightenment.

Jodee frankly admits he's not sure why his place is so popular but reckons it's because he offers good food at good prices.

"Food is my life," he says. "I have a genuine concern for my product and for the needs and desires of my customers."

It's more than that, however. You can get a pretty good meal at similar or better prices nearby without waiting in line.

The mystique of the name may be part of it.

Returning tourists say they make it a point to stop at the restaurant on their island vacations and newcomers feel obliged to visit a world-famous place when they have the opportunity.

The "World Famous" part of the name was Jodee's own idea, added 15 years ago when he took over the little Breakfast Club restaurant previously operated by his mother.

"A professor who taught a business course at the Culinary Institute in New York said everyone in here is world famous because it's impossible to disprove," Jodee laughs, noting that this statement was about all he remembers from that class.

"That always stuck with me and as soon as I took the place over a Gypsy-type sign painter came through and I told him to paint me the biggest ass carnival type

Jodee Sadowsky at work in his World Famous Breakfast Club.

sign he could with those words on it, and I slammed it up there. I think it cost me fifty bucks. I bought the plywood. The sign upset a lot of people, but they couldn't disprove it."

Given its present popularity and the thousands of world travelers who have eaten there, it might be possible to prove the place has grown into its name, and its proprietor has become somewhat famous himself.

Jodee was picked to handle chef's duties for one of the most exclusive weddings in recent memory, John F. Kennedy Jr.'s nuptials at Greyfield Inn on Cumberland Island.

"They wanted someone who could think on their feet and make do with a minimum of resources, someone who could work quickly and efficiently with a smile on their face and get along with folks," he says. "It was a very tight group. They wanted someone to break the ice."

"I had a blast. I worked 18 or 19 hours a day. I was only supposed to do a small amount of work, but I wound up taking over."

Far from working with few resources, Jodee says "they had ordered gross amounts of food. Every refrigerator was just filled to the brim with everything. Some of the items I'd never seen before."

"It was very hard work, with long days and long hours but as you worked, since the kitchen at Greyfield Inn is central, the guests would come and go, and you couldn't tell the guests from the workers."

Jodee says he was surprised, "being a conservative and spending a weekend with a bunch of liberals and waiting on them hand and foot, to find them to be very thankful and gracious."

"I was treated very well and so was everyone else, across the board. They didn't hesitate to ask questions or converse on a personal level. We made a lot of small talk. I was shocked."

On the day the newlyweds departed they got Jodee up at 4 a.m. to prepare their breakfasts, and he wound up chatting with them quite cozily as he cooked.

"We talked about football and all kinds of neat things," he says.

Once finishing their meal, the Kennedys vanished almost instantly.

"They took off on a boat or a helicopter or whatever and got the hell out of Dodge," says Jodee, then, reflecting, adds: "It would be cool if they showed up at the Breakfast Club one day."

That's pretty heady stuff for a kid who left his home just outside Chicago at 18 and headed up the highway with no plans, no money, and no preconceived destination.

Jodee had been, and remains, a self-starter his entire life.

When he was just 7, he worked around his aunt's tavern in the rough, tough southside Chicago area, cleaning up and arranging goods behind the bar.

"That was my first exposure to the work ethic," he says. "I'd go over there with my older brother and sister, and we'd be put to work right away. I swept the floor a lot better than they could, and I was put to work stocking the bottles."

While still a kid, he worked on farms southwest of the city and was once hired to groom, feed, and water the famous Budweiser horses, later expanding his chores to cleaning the barns and stables where the mammoth animals were housed.

When he got a bit older, he worked in several Chicago pizza parlors.

Jodee's early inculcation of the work ethic made him a success behind the pizza ovens.

He recalls doing "pretty good at that work and making a lot of money at it. After a couple of months, they would let two people go because I was doing the work of three."

Following his parents' divorce, while still working and attending high school, he became the principal housekeeper for his father, an airline pilot, in their large suburban home.

"It generally required about 40 hours of labor a week," he says. "I was a teenager doing laundry, dishes, and housework, and going to school and working on the side. I was a busy boy."

That hectic schedule, and his concern that he might get caught up in the burgeoning drug scene which had entrapped so many of his buddies, ultimately got "to be too much and I dropped out of school at 18 and headed out of town on foot," he says. "That was May 16, 1976."

After walking north for a day and a half with no food and no money, he spotted a red, white, and blue U.S. Army recruiting van and went inside to ask for help.

The next thing he knew he was in basic training at Ft. Knox, Kentucky.

Jodee's proclivity for hard work and respect for organization paid off again when he donned a uniform.

"I loved the army," he says. "I love the military life. It was very structured. Things were spelled out. They were very well organized. It was a wonderful thing when you were 18 with no place to go."

Jodee excelled at soldiering and was screened out of basic training after only a couple of months, given two rapid promotions, then underwent Special Forces training and became a Green Beret.

He was stationed in Panama at the time President Carter signed the agreement to turn the canal over to that country.

"That was one of the most interesting, challenging, and rewarding times of my life," he says. "Someday I might go back. I loved it. That's where I discovered who I was and what I was capable of doing."

Jodee was promoted to E5 (sergeant) in under three years.

"Unfortunately, I got transferred to the 82nd Airborne

Division at Ft. Bragg, which was short of personnel at the time," he says. "I made 76 jumps but I discovered right away that I wasn't going to be as successful as I thought I could be."

Frustrated, he applied for admission to the prestigious Culinary Institute of America in New York "because I was always really good at cooking, was always faster than any of my co-workers and felt I could make a career of it."

Once accepted, he opted out of the army after three and a half years.

While at the institute he learned pastry preparation, baking, food management, menu writing, building design, accounting "and just about everything you could ever imagine," he says.

His first job after completing culinary training was in Tucson, Arizona where he was hired as assistant kitchen manager for a franchise restaurant.

"It was a great place with great people, but the owner gave his buddies the good jobs," says Jodee.

The best thing about that job occurred when he was surprised to find Cheryl, an old acquaintance, right there in the restaurant.

They had grown up together in Chicago, where they went through catechism together and served as officers of the same high school class.

Back then, they were just friends, having dated only once over the years, but their attraction was dramatically different this time around. They married shortly after meeting again.

"We both needed something when we met again in Tucson, and we've been together ever since," smiles Jodee. "She's the Big Kahuna, not me. She's the one who straightened me out. If it hadn't been for her, who knows where the hell I'd be."

Ultimately, he was promoted to the position of kitchen manager in the chain's Phoenix restaurant, but he moved on because that job left something to be desired as well.

Jodee was subsequently employed by several restaurants, including one in the big Marriott Hotel on Michigan Avenue in Chicago.

"That was cool," he says. "It was a huge, institutional kitchen, and that's where I learned a lot and honed my skills."

Later, he handled a large kitchen for a Holiday Inn in Tempe, Arizona.

"They had virtually no employees and I was cooking breakfast, lunch, and dinner," he recalls. "I'd go through a pair of shoes in a month. The food business is rough."

While in Arizona, Jodee got a call from his mother, Helen, who said she was about to sell the little Tybee restaurant she had operated since 1976, along with a sandwich shop she opened later across the street.

"I had just landed a great job and had gotten a nice apartment and things were looking really good, but I asked her to give me a shot at it," Jodee recalls. "We

Jodee discusses early days in kitchen.

talked for two or three hours, and we settled on some ideas about how we would handle it, and she said OK."

"I was out of there and headed to Tybee with everything I owned in a U-Haul. I ran out of gas at a sign saying it was 11 miles to the island with only seven cents in my pocket."

"I had to panhandle a quarter from a cop to call Helen to come and get me. She came with a gas can, and when I got to the island, after driving for hours, I sacked out. Six hours later, she got me up and said it was time to get to work."

Jodee has been working ever since, at one point going almost four months without a day off.

His mother had made many friends and was doing relatively well at the restaurant, but once he took over and added "World Famous" to the name, business skyrocketed.

His hard work, outstanding cuisine and the force of his gregarious personality helped transform the place into what is by far the most popular breakfast establishment on Tybee.

Helen continued to work in the restaurant for a while, then moved to a large estate she had purchased in Florida for several years before returning to Tybee. She's now employed by her son and "at 72 she can still work circles around everybody else," says Jodee.

He has expanded and renovated the restaurant three times and recently acquired an adjoining building on Butler Avenue.

Along the way, Jodee's culinary ingenuity has resulted in unique dishes which have been written up in books and national publications, including the New York Times.

"But for a while there, all I did for a long time is work, work, work, and try to think about how to improve the place," he says.

"For the first three years, I was the only cook, a one man show. I was part of the frying pan, standing there like an octopus. It took a tremendous amount of concentration and preparation. It was extremely intense. Sometimes I'd get in there at 4 in the morning and by 11 my brain wasn't working anymore.

"My wife does all the thinking now. She's one of those behind-the-scenes workers who doesn't get appreciated. She works more hours than I do. Our house is her office, and she does all the accounting and has done a darn good job for us and our family."

Jodee also attributes his growing clientele to his fellow chef, Joel Worth, who he says "can make an old boot taste good. He may not make it look pretty. I can make things look pretty, but I don't care what you give this fella, he's one of the best I've ever met."

Reflecting on his enormous success, Jodee says while he always hoped, and to some extent anticipated, he would be a success, "I never visualized having 35 people standing at 45 degrees in a 40-knot gale waiting to get into my restaurant."

"Are they crazy or what? I would never do that. You can go to the Tybee Market and get yourself a box of

Total and a gallon of milk and a paper."

Another factor which has likely contributed to his success is his credo:

"I have one motto, do unto others as you would have them do unto you, period," he says.

"I take pride in taking a loser and developing any ability he may have. I've got three guys out there in charge of their own kitchens who never cooked a lick in their lives. I'm probably prouder of that than anything else."

While he makes no show of it, Jodee has helped many islanders who were down on their luck. Once back on their feet, most have become regular customers.

Casting bread on the water frequently brings handsome returns.

One of the main problems the Breakfast Club and other island businesses have nowadays is finding low-cost labor, according to Jodee.

"I predicted that five years ago," he says. "Tybee is suffering what Hilton Head went through."

"They built themselves out of a labor force, and now, with high rents, there are no $250 to $450 monthly apartments left. They built them out. They woke up one day and found they had no cashiers, no bus boys, no waitresses, no cooks, and now it's happened to us. We're in the middle of it right now."

"Tybee has changed, but I'm not so sure we've improved. I don't like seeing change for the sake of change. That's what got Clinton elected. I don't want to hear change. I want to hear improvement. Let's make it better than it was."

Jodee is now considering opening a lunch and dinner restaurant in the adjoining building.

Aiming to share his knowledge with a wider audience, he is also putting together a sequence of culinary videos, using the gourmet kitchen he installed in his home as the set for the filming.

POSTSCRIPT: Jodee Sadowsky's World Famous Breakfast Club has been written up in numerous national publications and has been named the best place in the Savannah area for breakfast. While he never did open that dinner restaurant, the breakfast and lunch crowds continue to stand patiently in long lines outside, rain or shine, waiting for a seat in his justifiably famous eating emporium.

Robin Arnsdorff -

Walking Girl Takes Life in Stride

Covers Tybee One Step At a Time

She's known as the "walking girl" and virtually everyone on Tybee Island either knows or knows of her.

She's Robin Arnsdorff, a shapely blonde who is... well...a walking advertisement for walking.

Power walking, that is.

That's what she does.

Robin strides the beaches and highways of Tybee, from the south end on Tybrisa out to Fort Pulaski and back, almost every day it's not raining, and sometimes when it is.

"I get caught in the rain when it starts after I do, and I just keep on walking," she says.

Robin gets in 12 miles on her walks, mostly along Butler Avenue and out U.S. 80, and insists on doing it at least five days a week unless the weather or work prevent it.

Robin Arnsdorff stretches before starting walk.

"I never want to go more than two or three days without my walk," she says.

Right now, she's between jobs, having just been laid off from her advertising position with Dixie Crystals due to the staff reduction there when the company changed hands.

The good part is that she can now walk when she chooses, picking spots between showers, generally in the early afternoon. The bad part is that she must now find another job, hopefully one that will permit her to walk at reasonable hours and is in advertising, or perhaps in physical fitness.

That's one of Robin's dreams - getting her certification as a personal trainer, then working for a fitness center or individual and ultimately starting her own physical fitness business.

"There's a lot of business around here, particularly on Wilmington Island, for personal trainers," she says.

Personal trainers are popular with "people who are not motivated themselves," according to Robin. "If they know someone is waiting for them at a scheduled time and they're going to get fussed at if they don't show up, they'll be there. They hire trainers to motivate them. Most people need someone to work with them, and many can't find friends of spouses who are willing to."

But she'll settle for another position in advertising. That's what she got her degree in at the University of Georgia, and it's where she has had most of her working experience.

Robin was born and raised in Rincon, where her parents still live. Her mother is principal of Rincon Elementary School, and her father is employed by a paper company.

She's been coming to the beach since she was a kid, her folks having always kept a place at the beach to get away.

And she's been living on Tybee since 1994, when her parents bought a house on the south end, and she offered to be their caretaker. The arrangement worked out well since her parents came to the beach only occasionally for weekends, and Robin was working in Savannah.

She is particularly pleased to be at the beach because it meshes perfectly with her penchant for walking.

"I feel safe there," she says. "I can walk any time of

the day or night and not have to worry about it. I couldn't do that in the city."

Occasionally, the attractive young strider encounters problems even at the beach, however, but she attributes them mostly to vacationers who are partying excessively.

"I had a man walk up to me on Butler as I passed and give me his room number at a motel - like I'd be interested in going there!" she frowns.

"He said, 'I'm in room 328, Baby' and I patted my sweatshirt and replied, I've got a .357, Baby, and he took off!"

Most times her major annoyance is men yelling at her from passing cars.

Robin figures they're just having a good time and maybe drinking too much, but she does carry pepper spray just in case and usually has her boyfriend, David Turner, who is also a walking enthusiast, along with her.

She was a pretty fair athlete in high school, serving as lifeguard at the New Ebenezer Retreat Center in Effingham County from the time she was a sophomore until she graduated, and during her freshman year at the University of Georgia she joined the Dolphin Club, a synchronized swimming group.

"That was a lot of work, a lot of exercise, and a lot of fun," she says.

Unfortunately, the program conflicted with her night classes the following year so she had to drop out.

Robin waves and smiles at passersby as she and David stride west on Highway 80.

It was in her freshman year that she put on a little weight.

"You know the freshman thing," she says. "Everybody gains some weight when they go to college."

It was the weight that led to the walking.

Robin enlisted her roommate, who needed to lose considerably more weight, as a walking partner and together they worked themselves up to two-mile strolls.

But that did little for Tybee's walking girl. She actually gained five or ten pounds.

So Robin extended her walks to six miles and lost her roommate's accompaniment in the process.

It was then that she started power walking although

"I really didn't know I was power walking until someone told me," she laughs. "I was just trying to walk really fast because I was by myself and I wanted to get home. I never had any instruction in it."

Robin says she had tried running and aerobics earlier, but they weren't for her.

"Walking relaxes me," she says. "I can get home from a horrible day at work, and go for a walk and when I get back, I don't even remember what the bad day was about.

"When I'd come home from running, I'd just be even more stressed out, plus my legs hurt."

It wasn't long before "six miles didn't seem like much, so I went on to eight and then ten miles," she says.

She continued walking after graduation when she moved to Statesboro to work in accounting for Belk's department store.

"I'd get up at 5:30 a.m. to walk before going to work," she recalls, but that ended when a policeman stopped her pre-dawn walk to inform her that a woman had been raped just a block away about the same time two nights earlier.

He suggested that she find a partner for her walks or take them in the middle of the day.

Since she could not walk at mid-day because of her job, Robin joined a gym and tried aerobics for exercise but suffered from shin splints "and I put on 13 pounds," she says. "I got up to 155 pounds!" (She now weighs 110.)

Shortly afterward, she returned to Rincon for a brief stint at teaching and took up walking again.

"I got up to 12 miles, and I lost 40 pounds, and I was still eating my mom's fried chicken," she smiles. "I didn't go on a diet. Walking did it for me when nothing else would.

"Working out in a gym just made me hungry. Walking will burn calories. It's a good way to get weight off. People see me at dinner, and they can't believe I eat that much. I eat a lot, and one of my hobbies is going to the sushi restaurant in Savannah. I've also got a thing about chocolate. I'll add a mile or two after I get into that."

Robin is convinced that walking is the way to go for healthy exercise.

She says "it's something you can do for your entire life, unlike a lot of other sports, and they say running is not good for women because it will jostle you around and

Robin's hair bounces jauntily as she follows David across Lazeretto Bridge.

mess up your insides.

"And walking is free! All you have to buy is your shoes."

She says she wears out a pair of shoes in about three months and usually buys the inflatable kind since they give her more heel support. She gets running, rather than walking shoes because "the walking shoes just don't cut it."

Robin left Rincon after a few months to take a job in advertising sales and copy composition with Savannah Scene magazine "but that was kind of touch and go because we were dealing with a lot of small shops that were going in and out of business and just doing seasonal stuff."

After that, she landed her job with Dixie Crystals, working first as a sales assistant, then moving up to the advertising department dealing with national print media and ad agencies.

She was with the firm for almost four years before she was laid off in the work force reduction.

Robin says she did a lot of walking on the beach when she first arrived but had problems with blisters "because when you walk that far on the beach the sand moves and your foot moves a lot more."

Beach walking was also limited by the tides to only two days a week when she was working because at high tide there is not enough room to walk.

"Sometimes the tide would come in half way through the walk, and you couldn't get back, but I love walking on the beach," she says. "It's beautiful. My favorite time to walk there is at sunrise."

She prefers summer walking because she can wear less clothing then.

"When I'm wearing a heavy sweatshirt and stuff in the winter, I don't get near as good a workout," she explains. "I can't swing my arms as much. I feel like I get a much better overall body workout in the summer. You're free to move more in the summer."

Robin says she has absolutely no problem maintaining her weight with her walking regimen, regardless of her hearty appetite, although she admits that David is an excellent cook who does not include many fatty dishes in his meals.

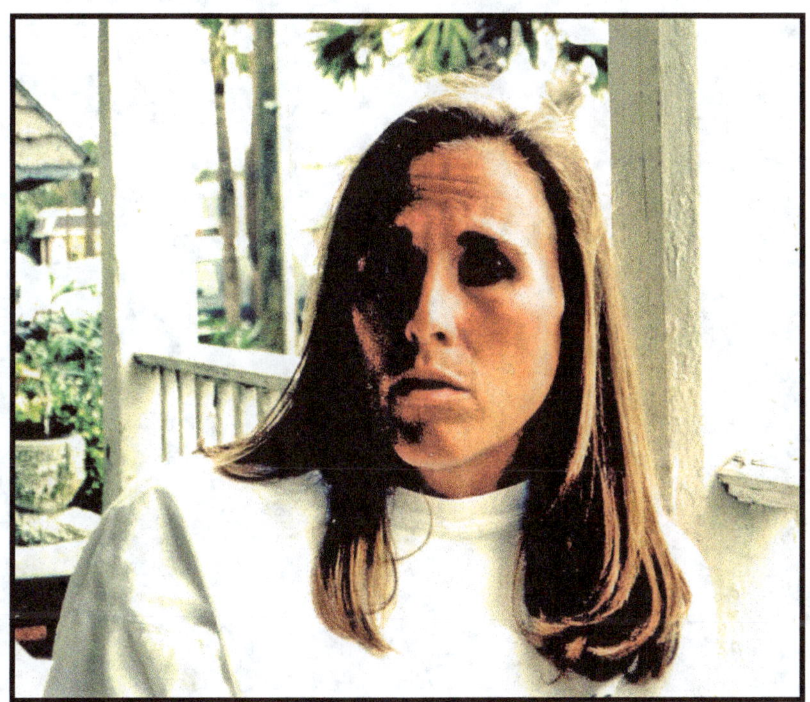

Robin relaxes after walk. It's wine time!

She also confesses to having wine with her meals, noting that she understands a glass of wine is good for the heart "so two must be twice as good!"

Happily, her beau is not only an excellent cook but an avid walker who accompanies her on most of her outings.

"That's one of my requirements for a boyfriend," Robin laughs.

Walking couple take a breather on the bridge.

She is pleased with her present selection, who is actually starting to out-walk her now.

"Men tend to be faster," she says. "David used to run a lot, but it was bad for his knees. This is great for him since it doesn't put that pressure on his knees."

But what she really wants to get is a large dog she can always count on as a walking companion.

"It has to be big and have long legs, though," she says, recalling an experience she had when she took a dog along on her walk awhile back.

"It was back in college, and I had a friend who had a pug dog she said really loved to walk for miles," laughs Robin.

"One day after walking my first six miles I stopped by to take the dog along for the last six. When we got four miles from the house, he laid down and would not move. He just lay there and moaned. That dog weighed 65 pounds, and I had to pick him up and carry him four miles back to the house. When I got back, I said I never want to see that dog again!"

Robin says she can't imagine ever giving up her walking routine and is hopeful she can find employment which will enable her to continue a good walking schedule.

There are a lot of islanders who hope she is successful.

Hundreds of people have become accustomed to seeing her walking beside Highway 80 each day, resolutely pumping her arms as her long blonde hair bounces jauntily with each stride.

Most wave and return her pleasant smile. Robin makes them feel good about the island, and themselves and she has inspired many a couch potato to waddle out for a brief stroll.

"Since I've been here, I see more and more people out walking each year," says Tybee's walking girl. "It's a good sign!"

POSTSCRIPT: Robin Arnsdorff never acquired that long-legged dog or her certification as a personal trainer but while it has been 26 years since this article was written, she continues to make her power walks around the island. Robin and David have opened their own computer firm on Tybee, making it possible to walk pretty much when they choose, and although David still accompanies her on most days he is no longer her boyfriend. "I married him because he could keep up with me," she smiles, while adding: "Anyway, Turner is a lot easier to spell than Arnsdorff!"

Jack Youmans - Keeping 'em Honest at City Hall

Old Politician Keeps Telling It Like It Is

He's grizzled, irascible, loveable, straight-shooting

Pick an adjective, you'll find someone to confirm it.

Despite their predilection, however, most islanders agree that "Mr. Tybee," the guy who keeps 'em honest at City Hall, is a fitting moniker for Jack Youmans.

The bewhiskered old coot (It's okay! Jack's an old-time politician who recognizes the value of publicity. He says you can call him anything and say whatever you want, as long as you mention his name) has set a modern-day record for consecutive terms on City Council - six, count 'em - and he's not done yet.

"Blatantly honest" is another fitting handle.

Just before the election one year, Jack told a crowd of about a hundred gathered for a "Meet the Candidate Night" at the Legion Hall that if they elected him, they could pretty much forget about his catering to the

Jack Youmans makes a point during city council meeting.

pressure they might bring at City Council meetings.

"Ladies and gentlemen, you're basically the same folks who attend most of our council meetings," he said. "But you're the minority. The majority of our people are at home - cooking, watching television, or sleeping. Keep in mind that if I'm elected, I'm supposed to represent all island residents, and I'm going to do just that!"

The group - far from being offended - placed Jack near the top of the candidates' list in a straw vote held just after his speech.

Jack's been winning island elections since 1986 and became mayor pro tem in 1990, when he garnered more votes than any other council candidate.

He doesn't do it by being circumspect.

Once, he answered charges by a self-righteous island

critic who claimed drugs and prostitution were rampant by stating that neither drug dealers nor prostitutes could make a living on Tybee because there was so much free stuff, they'd go broke.

"Any prostitute who came to the island from Savannah for a weekend would have to borrow money to get back to town," said Jack.

And he'd know.

Jack's not always been the sedate 70-year-old gentleman he appears as he sits in his sign and locksmith shop on Tybee's north end.

He built and operated several bars on what was a rather naughty south-end strip (16th Street, cum Tybrisa) in the old days, when you could keep a bar open 24 hours a day.

"You talk about crowds? We had 'em," he says, recalling the time when he ran the now defunct Mouse Trap Bar on Butler Avenue.

"If you didn't have a stool by one 1 o'clock on Saturday or Sunday afternoon, you wouldn't get one," he says. "And fights? We had 'em from inside the bars all the way down 16th Street.

"We didn't call the cops. There were only four of 'em, including the chief, and the crowd was covering the streets.

"I only called the cops for a fight one time. They told me that if I couldn't handle the fights inside the bar, they'd just close the place down. They'd handle the stuff outside, but we had to take care of it in the bar."

In those days his bar had go-go dancers, and Jack not only managed the place but kept three houses out back for the girls.

"Seems like we had a lot more fun back then," he says.

But don't get the wrong idea. Jack says he didn't mess with the girls he employed. He was too busy with his own girlfriends.

"I had two girls at the time, one in town and one at the beach," he says. "They kept me pretty busy, and it was real good 'til the beach girl found out about the one in Savannah. I lost 'em both!"

Jack also ran a little gambling operation on Lazaretto Creek for a while.

Neither those extended bar hours nor the gambling were strictly legal, but nobody much cared back then.

He recalls when Jimmy Carter was running for governor and came down to reassure island bar owners that their extraordinary hours - "We just had to close one hour before sunrise services one day a year," says Jack - were no problem.

"He told us that no state authorities would bother us during his administration.

"I voted for him, and not three months after he was elected 52 state troopers swooped down on Tybee and closed all the bars for being open after midnight on Saturday. They arrested all the bartenders and owners; loaded us all on a school bus and hauled us off to the Chatham County jail."

After that incident, Jack gave up the bar business and started his sign shop.

Carter, incidentally, didn't get his vote when he ran for re-election.

While many think Jack's been on the island forever, he's really been a resident for only 35 years or so.

And if you're a constituent and looking for him in the phone book, you'll need to find the name John Q. Youmans.

Years back, an acquaintance charged a whopping bill to his phone, and Jack informed the phone company he refused to pay it. They said if he didn't, they'd disconnect his phone.

He didn't. They did.

Jack solved the problem by having his phone reinstalled later under the name John Q. Youmans, and it's been listed that way ever since.

He's originally from Savannah, where he lived with his family in a large house on Habersham Street through his teen years.

Jack got into a spot of trouble there, as well, when he was 18. Three years later, however, he received a

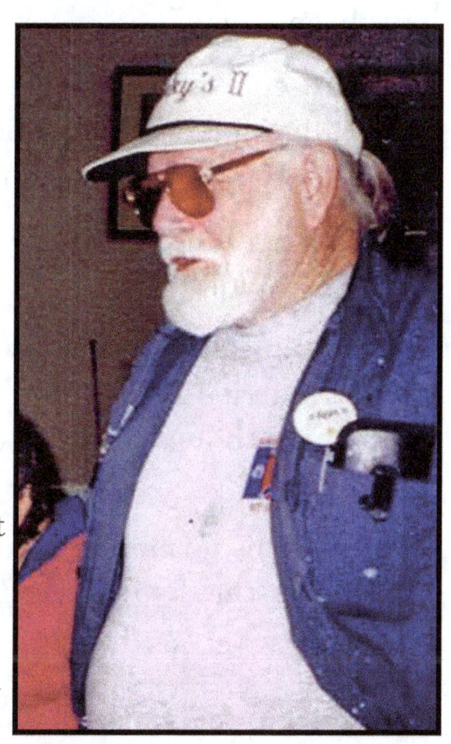

Jack talks politics.

full pardon. Since then, there's been nary a blemish on his record.

As a teen he also did a short stint in the Merchant Marines before joining the Air Force and serving in Korea.

Somewhere in there Jack got married. He remained that way for 20 years and a pair of kids. The divorce was not what you'd call amicable.

His former wife, Marguerite, got the big house, the second largest residence on Causton Bluff at the time.

When Jack showed up to retrieve the extensive set of Mercury outboard tools he kept in his workshop (he was a top hydroplane boat racer on the Southeast Circuit at the time) Jack said, "she claimed they must have been stolen".

On a subsequent visit to his former home to retrieve a .38 caliber pistol he had left there, Jack says he was surprised to find a male acquaintance in residence.

After letting him in, the guy got pretty antsy, according to Jack, and said:

"Before you say anything, we just want you to know we was married Friday. Nothing was goin' on before the divorce though, and we don't want anyone to think there was."

Turns out his former wife married the fellow just 16 hours after the divorce was final, Jack says.

His response?

"Well, if anybody asks, I won't tell 'em nothing but that you had the shortest f....ing courtship in the world!"

It was six years before Jack spoke to the pair again.

Time, however, heals most wounds. Now they all get together, including his second wife, Cathy, and their child, for family holidays at Marguerite's current house on Wilmington Island.

Cathy, to whom he is still married, is a cop in Thunderbolt. Jack was 42, Cathy 19 when they wed. They've been married for almost 30 years but are now separated.

When they went in to agree on the divorce, Jack says the lawyer, a mutual friend, observed that they really didn't seem like they wanted to take that final step.

"We signed the papers, and he agreed to keep 'em in his safe and if either one of us called to say we wanted the divorce, he'd process 'em," says Jack.

The papers have remained in the safe for six years now.

Jack says Cathy is really his best friend now. They frequently bring one another gifts and call on one another

Jack on the campaign trail.

when they have a problem, in addition to getting together for those big family gatherings.

This doesn't mean it's always been sweetness and light, however.

Once, after he attended a Chatham County municipal meeting in Thunderbolt and had sipped two or three liquid beverages, Jack was driving back toward Tybee when he spotted his wife's cruiser behind him on the bridge over the Wilmington River.

"I was driving real careful, and I was alright. Hell, at that time I could handle 20 drinks and have no problem, and I'd only had a couple. I was driving straight between the lines, not speeding or anything."

At that moment, however, his companion grabbed him in an unmentionable location and "I started weaving all over the bridge," says Jack.

Suddenly the lights of the cruiser started flashing, and his wife pulled him over.

A heated exchange followed, during which Cathy demanded that Jack and his friend get out of the car and leave it on the side of the road. After further conversation, during which Jack loudly proclaimed his innocence, Cathy drove him and his friend to Tybee. Jack had to get a ride back to retrieve his vehicle the next day.

"You talk about a mad human being," says Jack, "That was me!"

Jack also recalls a time, two years after their separation, when Cathy called him aside after another meeting in Thunderbolt.

"She said she just wanted me to know - before I heard it somewhere else - that she had decided to start dating," Jack says, laughing with the recollection.

"I said, Honey, I thought we decided to do that two years ago. If we didn't, I'm in a whole pecka trouble!"

Now, his life has pretty much settled down at Tybee, running his sign shop and serving as the island's curmudgeon councilman.

Jack's given up smoking, watches his diet, and has only an occasional drink. He's even got his old Harley up for sale.

He says he has no aspirations to be mayor of Tybee - "I think that job calls for someone with a little more tact than me" - but he does intend to continue running

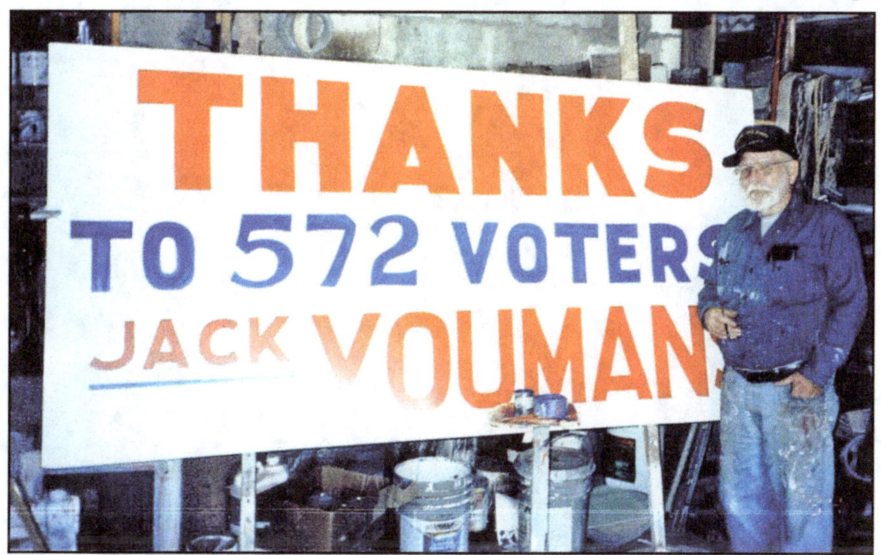

Jack creates sign to thank constituents after winning council seat again.

for his long-term council seat.

"I'll keep running as long as my health holds up," he says, noting that he feels "as good as I did ten years ago.

"I've told some close friends to keep an eye on me, and if I ever look like I've lost it - like I don't know what I'm doing - to tell me, and I'll get out of there."

That would be Tybee's loss. It's hard to imagine the island without "Mr. Tybee" keeping 'em honest down at City Hall.

POSTSCRIPT: John O. (Jack) Youmans moved to Richmond Hill, Georgia after serving on Tybee's City Council for 18 years. He passed away on March 31, 2012. Jack was 87.

Spec Hosti -

Women Always Surround Councilman

"Spectacular" Is The Name for This Troubadour

Tybee's troubadour City Councilman Michael Hosti, who is far better known as "Spec," has been surrounded by women his entire life.

This is not to say that he's a philanderer, although word has it that he was right popular with the women as a young man.

Now 46, he still looks like a teenaged beach boy with his rail-thin frame, dark tan, and long hair pulled back in a ponytail.

Blessed with a deep and melodious southern drawl, Spec admits he got along pretty good with the ladies in his early days.

"I dated all the prettiest girls on Tybee, but I married the prettiest one of all," he says.

Liking the girls came naturally since he has always been surrounded by women. He's the only boy in a family of seven girls, all of whom still live on the island.

His marriage in 1974 simply increased the distaff population since he and his wife, Debra, have one child who is - what else? - a girl.

In addition to her good looks, Spec says Debra "is a good cook and a master gardener."

He says he enjoyed almost every minute of his youth with his horde of sibling sisters, save for the fact that his friends accused him of being spoiled because he was the only boy in the family.

"Man, those guys didn't know what they were talking about," he claims. "My sisters were tough."

Incidentally, he picked up the nickname "Spec" in grade school when he got a monstrous hit in a softball game.

Spec Hosti beside the moat at Ft. Pulaski.

"That's spectacular!" one of his teammates exclaimed, and he's been called Spec ever since.

"A lot of the folks who saw me as a kid think it came from all the freckles I had then though," he laughs.

Spec is also surrounded by dozens of Hosti relatives, the family being one of the oldest and most populous on the island.

Although his father, Ernest C. Hosti, was born in Europe, his mother's side of the family has deep southern roots. Her name was Dorothy Helen Lee, and her family has traced its lineage back to Robert E. Lee.

Spec attended St. Michael's School on Tybee before spending a year at St. John Vianney Minor Seminary on Isle of Hope in Savannah when he was considering entering the priesthood.

"But I discovered girls, and it changed all that," Spec grins.

Then he completed three years at Benedictine Military School and a year at the Savannah Vocational School.

His troubadour persona stems from his popularity as a mandolin player. He and his band, "The Flying Sheepheads," perform regularly at Shorty's Round Table and the Wind Rose Cafe, among other spots on the island.

The band - featuring Dobby Simmons on bass, John Kellam on fiddle, and Virgil Graham on guitar, in addition to Spec - plays an interesting combination of country-rockabilly with strong bluegrass underpinnings.

Spec checks repairs at Cockspur Light.

Their renditions of "Fox on the Run," "Good Hearted Woman," "Goin' Back to Georgia," and "Bar-B-Que," are something special.

Music has been a mainstay of Spec's life since he was a kid. First, he learned to play a harmonica, then a guitar, and finally, his real love, the mandolin.

A friend, Herby Weaver, brought a mandolin down to the beach years ago, and Spec took to it immediately. He purchased an instruction book and started playing the instrument, then going to bluegrass festivals, and has continued perfecting his technique ever since.

Recently, he's written a number of songs and is considering putting together an album and hopes to expand The Flying Sheepheads' horizons.

"Honestly though," he says, "I just want to be involved in music in whatever capacity."

His day job is managing the maintenance department at Ft. Pulaski, where he's been employed for 25 years with the National Park Service.

"What I'd really like" in connection with that job "is to be superintendent" of the fort, he says, noting that he gave up the idea of moving around the country with the Park Service long ago when his wife, who was born on the island, made it clear she did not want to stray far from Tybee.

Given his occupational progression at the fort - he started out as a temporary laborer, then became a maintenance worker, and then a carpenter before being named maintenance chief - he should have a realistic shot at that position.

Spec is on the job at Ft. Pulaski.

Several years ago, Spec became interested in politics and decided to run for a seat on city council.

The first time out he failed to garner enough votes, although some suggested wryly that he had enough votes in his family alone to be elected.

Spec's response was, "Heck, I don't even know if my sisters voted for me."

There may be more truth than fiction to this observation since one of his sisters was also a candidate in that election.

The second time out he won a seat handily, garnering the second highest vote total of all the candidates, though he points out that his sister didn't run in that election.

His approach to electioneering was about as typical as Spec's approach to most things...something like chilling out in a hammock on a hot summer day.

"I didn't spend a penny on the campaign for council," he says. "As a matter of fact I didn't even put up a campaign poster until two days before the election, and then I put up only two signs and they were back to back."

Spec reckons he'll saunter (running just doesn't seem to fit this guy) for a council seat again when his present term expires, since he finds the position kind of interesting.

Likely, he'll be successful… unless all his sisters decide to run. In any event the effort should be cheap at the price.

***POSTSCRIPT:** After leaving his Council seat for several years Spec concentrated on his music and regular job at Ft. Pulaski. Following his retirement he became co-owner of the Cockspur Grill on Tybee in 2020 and made another successful run for City Council. Meanwhile, Spec and his band continue to play at various venues throughout the area.*

Judy Helmey -
The Matriarch of the Fleet

A Real Princess of Tides

Judy, Judy, Judy.

While that may sound like a bad Sammy Davis Jr. impersonation of Cary Grant, it's not. What it is is a long list of boats, people, and dogs at the Helmey homestead on Wilmington Island.

Judy Helmey is the matriarch of the Judy dynasty.

Her dog's name is Judy, and her charter fishing boat is the Miss Judy, as was her previous boat and the dozens before that. They were always Miss Judy, unless they were Miss Jerry, named for Judy's mother.

An attractive, bronze-skinned athletic woman with a smile as wide as the Savannah River, Judy keeps the current Miss Judy tied up at a dock down a path from the house where she's lived her entire life.

She's been operating boats from that site since she was a child. While still in her teens, she became the youngest certified female charter boat captain in the Southeast. Her father, Sherman I. Helmey, operated boats from the same site.

It was he who got her started.

"When I was only about six," Judy recalls, "I'd take the helm on his big boat while he took a nap as we headed back in from the fishing grounds." ("Back in" was usually a 70-mile ocean run from beyond the Snapper Banks east of Tybee Island.)

"Dad would tie a string from one of the spokes on the wheel and line it up with the compass at about 270 degrees. He said when I wanted to go north to go two spokes to the right of that. Two spokes to the left and I'd be turning south. That's how I learned to read a compass."

On fishing trips, he had Judy put her own line out one of the windows in the cockpit. "When he'd come to a school of fish, he'd turn the boat so my line went through before the others. I'd always catch the first fish," she laughs. "Everyone thought I was the fisherman of all fishermen! I learned to love to fish."

Judy and her father, a well-known colorful and charismatic character, were clearly a very close crew.

In the old days, she used to stay up all night with him, bailing out his wooden boats after they'd waited for the wood to swell after caulking between the planks. It was quite a chore since "we didn't have automatic bilge pumps then," she recalls.

Early on, he advised her never to try to follow another boat in saying, "If you don't know where you're go-

Judy Helmey discusses family and fishing.

ing, why the hell do you think the guy in front of you does?"

He taught her a lot of other important stuff as well, like what to do when you're caught at sea in a waterspout.

"Don't try to run through the spout," Judy quotes her father as telling her. "It's a wall of water going straight up, and it'll tear you up. Stay inside it and run as fast as you can in a direction counter to the spout's direction."

While this might seem like gratuitous advice to most of us, it served her well several years ago, just after she purchased the current 34-foot fiberglass Miss Judy.

She was returning from a day's fishing with a group aboard, when the weather radio advised getting off the water.

"The sea was rising with five-to six-foot waves, no big deal, but there were heavy clouds to port and starboard," Judy recalls. "The radar was filled with them, but I saw a clear spot at least a mile wide between 'em, and I was running for it.

"Then, suddenly, a waterspout formed, either under me or over me. I was in the middle of it! The water was churning, and I started running the boat as fast as I could, turning hard, opposite the direction of the spout, keeping the bow into the waves.

"Lightning was all… ALL AROUND US! The boat was right inside it. The lightning was right here, not out there! The wind gauge stopped working when the wind speed hit 60 knots. The top of the boat blew off, and all the instruments were smashed. And those were stainless fastenings holding the top on.

"It seemed like hours, but in about ten minutes the thing just lifted, and was gone."

Her passengers were still huddled, praying, when the spout lifted. Miraculously, no one was injured.

Her dad was quite a guy, she says, and he taught her well.

Sherman married seven times, once for only six weeks.

His second wife, Jerry, was Judy's mother. Before heading to sea, he owned the old Trailways Bus Station in Savannah, now the site of the Chatham County Court House, along with several automotive repair shops in the city.

And back in the 1930s he became a pal of notorious gangster Al Capone.

Judy says her father used to keep hotel rooms all over the area for Capone and his cronies when they came down to pick up bootleg liquor brought in by boat or for meetings with other mobsters at the old Oglethorpe Hotel on Wilmington.

He met Capone one evening, when the racketeer and another man drove a truck loaded with vegetables in to Sherman's shop near the Bradley Lock and Key store in Savannah.

"Capone's truck needed repairs. My father looked at the truck and told them it was still under warranty and they should take it to a General Motors dealer. They said no, they wanted him to fix it.

"Then they went into his restroom and changed into tuxedos and asked him to bring the truck around to a nearby hotel when the repairs were completed. Dad said the mechanic he assigned to the job got drunk. It was then that he discovered the bootleg booze under the load of vegetables.

"Dad worked all night to complete the repairs and then delivered the truck. He spent some time with Capone, and they became friends. He said Al Capone was a nice man."

That relationship lasted until the end of Prohibition.

Helmey handled modification work on Capone's fleet of "shoe salesmen's cars," picking them up in Chicago and driving them to Savannah to do the work. The pseudonym for the bootlegger's cars was based on the booze they stashed in containers that looked like shoe boxes.

"Dad would pick the cars up in Chicago, drive them down here and beef up the suspension so they wouldn't look like they had a load on 'em when they were carrying the liquor," says Judy. "He'd use leather and felt hats to stiffen the springs. They had all sorts of hidden compartments to hold the liquor."

Special markings on the tires let local authorities know who the cars belonged to.

"Everyone in the area knew what was going on," Judy says.

In addition to renting Capone and his cronies scores of rooms, many for a year at a time, Sherman frequently joined them for excursions on their yachts.

"They'd hold meetings on 'em all up and down the waterway," Judy remembers her father telling her. "They'd pick up booze at a place called Star Island, off Florida."

Those boat trips apparently whetted her father's appetite for the sea, since he entered the charter boat fishing business after Prohibition ended, and Capone's arrest for income tax evasion severed his connection with the mobster.

Judy relaxes on boat while recalling fish stories.

Sherman bought the waterfront property on Wilmington Island in 1949. Meanwhile, he exhibited a hearty appetite for heavy drinking, partying, and women, and became a familiar figure at area bars.

"He got pretty loud when he was drinking and would clear a place out or be cleared out," says Judy. "Every place but Johnny Harris Restaurant on Victory Drive. They put up with him for some reason.

"And my father was kind of eccentric. He made arrangements with the highway department one time to get a bunch of that yellow paint they line the roads with. "He painted his entire boat with that stuff. His boat was always yellow."

"Everybody liked him. He was not only a lady's man but a real man's man."

Once, when she was taking a male customer out on her own boat at age 15 while her father was ferrying another party, the guy started fishing around with Judy instead of those in the water. She called her father on the boat's radio to tell him about the problem, and Sherman followed her back to their dock.

"When he pulled up to the dock, he stepped off the boat; never tied it up or anything. The boat ran itself off into the weeds. The dock was a real mess when Dad got through with that guy."

Judy has written one book about her father, and she's now working on another.

Although he's gone now, having passed away four years ago at age 94, she says he's still hanging around her place - and so is her mother.

Judy claims a handyman who cleans the Miss Judy asked recently about the man he frequently sees on the riverbank. When Judy asked for a description, the boat cleaner said the man's "always wearing khaki trousers and a white T shirt and smokes a cigar, but he's always gone when I try to talk to him."

Judy asked the handyman to wait a moment while she went to the house. She returned with a photo of her deceased father. "That's him!" the handyman exclaimed.

Other visitors frequently ask her about a dark-haired woman they see around the house. The woman they describe is, without question, her mother, says Judy. Her mother died in an automobile accident when Judy was five. She was buried on Nov. 13, Judy's birthday,

40 years ago.

"Funny thing about mother is that almost all the photographs I have of her were taken in cemeteries," says Judy. "She'd be smiling and leaning against one of the monuments or headstones."

Judy, who was an only child, believes the spirits of her father and mother are staying around to protect her.

"Often, I'll go into a room and know that a presence has just been there. The only really bothersome thing is the loud music and the smoke that fills the house in the middle of the night. They wake me up, and I can't go back to sleep. Sometimes it bothers me so much I turn all the lights on."

Judy says her father, in his last years, used to tell her about the loud party music he'd hear in the middle of the night, but she figured at the time he was imagining it.

"This place ought to be on the ghost tour!" she laughs.

Out on her charter boat, Judy is much more composed. But while she is definitely the captain and very much in charge, she says she feels she is working for her customers.

"They're my boss when I take them out. I try to find out what their needs are, what they want, and what makes them happy. I really enjoy it."

From the large number of her repeat customers, with more than 30 percent booking reservations a year in advance, she seems to be doing things right.

Judy stands tall aboard the current Miss Judy.

And, while facing rough weather - "when you're making a 140-mile round trip to the fishing grounds, you can't control changes in that," - she's rarely gotten in trouble. Even on those occasions when she does encounter an ominous situation, the customers don't know it.

"I'm always very calm," she says. "I'm responsible for them."

After being around the water her entire life and taking out fishing parties since she was 14, Judy has developed a lot of confidence at sea.

She carries enough fuel to make the 140-mile trip and still have 40 percent left in her tanks. She knows just where the fish are running and, be it in a favorite fishing spot six miles off shore, out on the Snapper Banks, or along the continental shelf, she'll find 'em.

Judy's knowledge is so respected that she writes weekly fishing reports for four publications in the area and collects specimens for the University of Georgia while her charter business keeps growing.

She plans to help design an even larger boat that will be built to her specifications in the near future.

Judy has even gotten into the burial business, since a growing number of people have requested that she bury relatives at sea.

"Some people request a sea burial before they die," she says. "They just want to be out there. Some have always dreamed of being at sea."

In response to such requests, Judy, accompanied by a

funeral home representative, ferries the body to a predesignated spot in about 60 feet of water, witnesses a special ceremony, and puts the weighted body overboard.

Judy, herself, never plans to be far from the sea. "I'll be doing this until I'm 150," she says. "Where else can you wake up knowing what you're doing, loving what you're doing, and getting paid for it? And it's not just a fishing trip. It's entertainment."

You'll always be able to find Judy the captain, Judy the dog, and whatever Miss Judy is currently in service down the dirt road just across from the May Howard School on Wilmington Island.

You might even bump into a couple of those Helmeys from the past.

POSTSCRIPT: Judy Helmey has become a leading authority on fishing in the coastal area. She now maintains a fleet of fishing vessels manned by a bevy of experienced captains and continues to write columns and articles with advice on inland and deep sea fishing for a number of area publications.

Joe Jackson -

Old Island Home Recalled as Close to Heaven

Childhood Memories Are Savored

Joe Jackson's close to God and heaven. Been that way all his life.

Maybe it's because he's so tall. Joe's six foot eleven, and that's a lot closer to heaven than some of us will ever get.

More likely it's because of his inherent spirituality and his family heritage. He was never far from a sermon. There's been a man of God, a preacher, in every Jackson generation.

Whatever it is, you can feel goodness around Joe. It's almost tangible.

Heaven for him, at least here on earth, is Bradley Point on Whitemarsh Island, just east of Savannah.

You'd know why if you spent a couple of hours walking around the area with him, letting his old memories filter through the morass of present-day problems. He emanates an ethereal aura as he strolls beneath the same moss-shrouded trees that were there when he was a boy.

"Sometimes I drive down here and just park," he says. "Sitting there, I can still hear my grandfather's voice calling 'Bubba' (Joe's childhood nickname)."

Joe always ran home from wherever he happened to be when he heard his grandfather call "Bubba!"

"I was always there by the time the 'ba' part of Bubba cleared his lips," he laughs. "I knew I'd better be."

Joe grew up on the point. From the porch of his house you could see the Wilmington River, Isle of Hope, Thunderbolt, Turner's Rock, and, across the marsh, on out to the ocean beyond.

That heavenly view is still there though the house is long gone.

Joe remembers every nook and cranny of the point as he walks, while sharing memories of what he believes was an idyllic childhood.

The old water oak from which he used to swing out over and into the river still stands, barren now and soon to be swallowed by the stream which is rapidly eroding the bank to which the old oak clings. Another nearby oak, which Joe guesses is nearly 200 years old, is still green, but it too has started to lean precariously toward the river.

He lingers to touch the remnants of a massive old fig tree planted by his great-great grandmother. As a child Joe plucked plump fruit from that tree, and although its huge trunk has now disappeared, he says the sprouts around it still bear delicious figs.

He stops to gaze into the waters of Negro House Creek, beside which his grandfather's oyster house once stood. Shells from those days still protrude from the bank beneath another massive oak where the oyster house squatted.

"I learned to swim in that creek," Joe recalls. "I had a theory of how it was done, but I'd never tried it."

One day he was out in a bateau with his grandfather when the old man suddenly pulled in his oars and threw Joe overboard before rowing off about 20 feet.

"When my head came up, I screamed 'I'm gonna drown!' He yelled, 'you aren't gonna drown; you're gonna swim'. And I did. I swam after that boat all the way to the mouth of the creek."

The entire area is now covered with ritzy houses surrounding the grounds of the Savannah Yacht and Country Club. Some lots sell for as much as a couple of hundred thousand dollars, and there must be several hundred houses there, most no more than a long putt from the one next door.

"All these people out here now," Joe muses. "They think they've got seclusion and what they want. Pretty soon, they're going to be living on top of one another."

When Joe lived here with his grandparents, there were only six families on the entire point. His grandparents had over eleven acres with a sweeping waterfront, large lake, and the oyster house from which his grandfather supplied area residents and Savannah stores.

While that now seems expansive, their homestead was small compared with those of their neighbors.

Joe says the Glendinning's had a spread that measured a mile by over two miles, stretching across to Commodore Point. Their old home now serves as the clubhouse for the yacht club.

Joe's was the only black family on the point. They had been there since Buster, his great-great grandfather, first settled in.

"It was heaven, my God, man, just heaven," says Joe. "I've got multimillion dollar memories."

He says he used to go out in the woods all alone and sort of listen to the Lord. "I'd sit there real quiet and catch the sound of the bluebird and the mockingbird and a bobwhite quail. Oh man, I was hearing God."

Joe has always had a feel for the sanctity of the site, but he had his share of fun there, too. He'd ride old Tom, his grandparents' horse, galloping through the woods pretending he was Zorro, at least until Tom decided he'd had enough and headed back home for some oats.

"He wasn't anything but an old hard-neck Carolina horse, but he sure was smart," says Joe, smiling as he reminisces.

"I'd take him out with a wagon to chop firewood, and he'd stay there when I dropped the lines. But he'd look over his shoulder once in a while as I loaded the wood and test the traces. When he leaned on those traces and thought there was enough of a load, you'd better be up there on that wagon 'cause he'd be headed off home in a hurry. He sure was a smart horse all right, and he was my friend."

Joe entertained himself before the days of television by knocking the spokes out of old wheels and rolling the rims around with a stick. And he'd make "pluff-ers." To make one, he says, "You take a hollow piece of bamboo and shove a teaberry in it with a wet broom handle. They'd shoot out of there with a bang. Sound-ed just like a pistol."

Back then the point was covered with mulberry trees, blackberries and blueberries, scuppernongs, chinqua-pins, figs, and yellow plums the size of golf balls.

"They were all part of our diet," says Joe. "Some kids today never heard of those things."

You won't find them on the point today. The place proliferates with roses, azaleas, and camellias. It's hard to find a chinquapin anywhere anymore, according to Joe, who says they belong to the acorn family and have prickly shells that pop open when they're ripe and "they're right good eating."

He says his family's four-acre lake "was filled with the biggest kind of mullet and trout and spotted-tailed bass."

Even the lake is gone now. They sealed off the old flood gates, and trees now grow where the fish once swam. "There'll soon be houses there too, I guess," sighs Joe.

In addition to frequent meals of fish,
his family trapped and ate raccoons.

Joe W. Jackson.
Photo from memorial service program.

"Coons 'er good eating as long as you know how to prepare 'em," he says. His grandmother knew how all right. "She could cook almost anything."

Joe says she used to have him put leftover fish out on the roof of the chicken shed to dry for a couple of days and then hang the dried fish up in the house for snacks.

"They never drew flies," marvels Joe, who says his wife now buys fish from the market, and when she puts the bag on the porch to return to the car for more groceries, flies are all over them before she gets back.

That, to Joe, is a simple proof that God takes care of those who place their faith in him.

His grandparents had ice delivered every two weeks and put 25 pounds of it in a tub in a hole behind the house, which they covered with burlap.

"There was still ice there when the next delivery was made two weeks later," he recalls, deeming this as another proof that God takes care of believers.

A considerably more graphic example was the hurricane of 1942.

"Winds were blowing through here at 125 knots," says Joe, who was seven at the time. "Limbs were sailing by like paper bags. It was the first time I'd ever seen the wind pop palm trees out by their roots. Trees were snapping all over the place."

His grandparents' house had a palm-thatched roof and was raised up off the ground on short stumps. "They weren't sunk in the ground," he says. "The house just sat on them.

"When I saw those trees snapping and palms popping, I figured that house was going to go. We had a long hall, open at both ends, with rooms off of it. My grandfather was just sitting there in a rocker with a Bible in his lap. He said, 'Bubba, go open the front door and the back door of the hall, and let the Lord come through this house'."

"And you know, nothing happened to that house. Not ne'er a single piece of thatch was blown away. Not one! When you place your faith in the Lord, He takes care of you. He'll spare you his wrath. The Lord'll hold you in his hands."

Joe's grandfather, John, was a preacher, as was Joe's father but his physical strength may have been almost as strong as his faith.

"He was a real mountain of a man," says Joe. "Seven foot two, and he wasn't fat. He was muscular; had huge arms."

In addition to being a preacher, John operated the oyster house and sailed out to the oyster beds in an 18-foot bateau he built himself.

Joe used to stand on the point and watch him sail in from Wassaw, out beyond the General Oglethorpe Hotel which is clearly visible from the old house site. His grandfather taught him how to build his own boat and weave casting nets by the time he was twelve; taught him to sail before he was nine.

"Kids just don't know that kind of stuff anymore," says Joe. "They sit around watching television now. Children today don't seem to have a sense of responsibility or character."

Back then the area offered a variety of wild food not only on land but in the surrounding waters, from which a wide variety of fish, huge blue crabs, and seemingly limitless oysters could be harvested.

Joe believes one of the reasons for their abundance is that his grandfather always returned the shells to the oyster beds.

"He'd mix cornmeal and mud with the shells, stir them

up, and then spread the mixture on the oyster beds at low tide. That provided food for the baby oysters, and they just kept on spreading."

His grandmother was the family medical practitioner.

Joe remembers the day he was killing time by balancing on a barrel while waiting for the school bus beside the highway to Savannah.

That spot was a mile from his house down a single-lane dirt road he had to walk going to and from the bus stop each weekday.

"I had 20 minutes to get to the house after getting off the bus," he says. "Whatever happened, that was the time I had. I always made it, walking or running."

Anyway, Joe was balancing on the barrel, rolling around while he waited for the bus, when it banged into a power-line pole, causing him to lose his balance and grab the pole as he slid down. Someone had left a razor blade in a seam in the pole, and it slashed his palm as he slid.

When he arrived at school, bleeding profusely, his teacher wrapped his hand in a cloth and sent him home, saying that she didn't have time to take him to a clinic.

It took three hours for him to get back home from the time of the mishap.

His grandmother inspected the deep gash and extracted the razor blade which was still embedded in his palm. Then she stuffed spider webs in the cut and packed it in red clay.

The wound healed so cleanly you'd never spot the hairline scar unless Joe pointed it out to you.

He also remembers that his mother, Latisha, suffered severe burns on her arm on two occasions. The burns on her forearm were treated at a Savannah hospital, and scars are still visible.

His grandmother treated equally severe burns on her upper arm using "mutton leaf," a plant which grew along the river bank.

She boiled the leaves and bathed the burn in the liquid, then wrapped it with the leaves. Joe says there's no evidence of that burn on his mother's upper arm.

He has other memories of that mile-long trek to the school bus as well.

One is about his grandmother always packing his lunch with four homemade biscuits and some fish, either whiting or mullet. By the time he walked the mile to the bus stop, the bag was greasy, and schoolmates would kid him about being a country boy with a greasy lunch bag.

To avoid the jokes, Joe started climbing an oak tree which still stands near the point road's intersection with Johnny Mercer Blvd. and stuffing the lunch bag in a fork of the tree before boarding the bus.

Fortunately, his grandparents gave him a quarter each day for spending money. His lunch throughout this period was milk and cookies purchased with that quarter.

While Joe may recall his childhood as idyllic, life at his grandparents' home seems more than a little harsh by modern-day standards.

When he arrived home from school, he would put on his work clothes, hitch up the horse, and plow until just before dark. After that, he'd go down to his grandfather's boat, help unload the oysters, and wash and shuck them.

"Then I'd walk back to the house, put on clean clothes and walk a mile to the Carson's house where I worked as a butler until about 9:00 or 10:00 p.m.," he recalls. "When I was finished, I'd walk back home and study until it was time to go to sleep."

Mornings, he was up at 4:00 to build a cooking fire for his grandmother. Then he'd put the horses and cows out to pasture before dressing and leaving for school.

"My day was a routine," he says. "I was always taught the value of work."

Joe has fond memories of the Glendinnings for whom he also worked. He says he was treated like a member of their family and felt like one.

"Robert Glendinning was a great man," says Joe. "He was a navigator and an aviator and a master carpenter."

They took him along on their frequent cruises on the Mystic, the 65-foot family yacht, and when he completed high school, he joined them on a six-month cruise to Nova Scotia.

Joe says Glendinning loaned him his car to take his date to his high school's senior prom and remembers how proud he was, noting, "It was a wood-sided station wagon, a real classic."

Glendinning drowned when he fell from a dock beside the Mystic in Jacksonville.

"When they called me and I went down there, it felt like something inside of me had died," he says.

"The people I grew up with had character. The Carsons, the Gibsons, the Demerys. I was a full-grown man before I knew there was a difference between blacks and whites."

While still attending Savannah State College, from which he graduated with a degree in engineering, Joe became an international longshoreman, a profession he pursued for the next 29 years.

He travelled the world many times over and conducted courses for shippers in Japan, Germany, Italy, and Australia.

"I was teaching them how to load their cargoes, so they would be easier to handle when they arrived in Savannah," he says. "I think I helped increase the ship traffic in the port here."

Joe also played a role in the construction of the Talmadge Bridge connecting Savannah to Hutchinson Island.

He says he conferred frequently with President Bush during the initial planning for the bridge, and, although he strongly supported the new span, it's not what Joe had envisioned.

"It's not high enough," says Joe. "They're going to

have to replace it, or the port won't be able to handle the ships of the future. They keep thinking if they dredge the channel deeper, it will take care of everything, but they've got to realize that when a ship isn't loaded, it rises high and won't be able to pass under that bridge."

One Japanese ship almost lost its antennae shortly after the bridge was built, he says.

Although Joe sailed to dozens of exotic ports during his years as a longshoreman, he was always drawn back to Bradley Point by his childhood memories.

"The shame is that soon nobody will remember what it was like in the old days," he says.

Now 62, Joe brings his grandson out to the point occasionally for picnics. They sit on ancient tree stumps, and Joe tells the boy what it was like when he was his age.

"I tell him how I used to sit real quiet in the turnip patch, and I could actually see them grow. You could see the earth move as a big turnip grew through it. I hope by telling him of those days, maybe it won't be forgotten. It was heaven, really."

Listening to Joe while watching the glow in his eyes, you can almost believe it. His spirit will be forever entwined with the moss swinging softly from the limbs of those massive old Bradley Point oaks.

POSTSCRIPT: The Rev. Joe W. Jackson passed away on May 9, 2021 at his home in Savannah. He

was 86 years old. That observation Joe made decades ago regarding the inadequate height of the Talmadge Bridge when it was initially designed seems prescient now with long-delayed plans underway to either raise or replace the structure to permit today's higher ships to pass underneath. Many of the larger ones must now wait for a low tide to make their passage. Meanwhile, his beloved old Bradley Point area has become pretty much a sea of "McMansions" with not a turnip patch in sight.

Mallory Pearce -
Councilman Covers Waterfront

Mixing Beer and Ecology

If you're a devotee of beachfront bistros, you won't have to look far to find one of Tybee's most flamboyant city councilmen.

Try any of the popular watering holes along the North End such as the old DeSoto Beach Hotel or Spanky's and you'll find him, brew in hand, chatting animatedly or dancing with one of his many constituents.

Mallory Pearce comes by the dancing naturally. His mother, Sally Pearce, built quite a reputation lighting up the DeSoto dance floor until the wee small hours.

"Usually she was dancing with much younger men," smiles Mallory.

His mother continued dancing until very late in life. She passed away two years ago at age 84.

Sally Pearce was also a noted artist and a founder of the Tybee Museum where her paintings are still on display. A popular Tybee figure, she was the first queen of the increasingly popular Beach Bum Parade and a vehicle is still entered in her honor in that annual harbinger of Tybee's summer beach season.

You'll be able to spot Mallory himself by his huge mane of salt and pepper hair, often protruding from the back of his frequently worn baseball cap as he meanders along the beach front at all hours.

Mallory is now 61 but he saunters like a young lion and does a wicked version of the Carolina shag with a variety of beach ladies of all ages who seek him out as a dance partner.

While the Pearce family has been a fixture at Tybee for years, and Mallory intends to keep it that way for the foreseeable future, they were originally from upstate New York, where they lived before moving to the beach in the 50s.

Mallory Pearce making the rounds on Tybee.

His father, George W. Pearce, was a noted chemist who, among other things, invented the No Pest Strip with fellow chemist Jim Miles.

Mallory says it's not true what they said in "The Book" (for the one or two people in the world who don't know, that's *Midnight in the Garden of Good and Evil*) that the "strip" was invented by a malcontent chemist who claimed his invention was stolen by his supervisor.

"My father was his supervisor, and he never stole anything," says Mallory.

His brother, Peter Pearce, now living in California, is well known as a furniture and structural designer.

Peter worked with furniture designer Charles Eames and designed the tandem chairs located in the Savannah Airport. He also worked with Buckminster Fuller on structural systems like the geodesic dome and was instrumental in the design of Biosphere II in Arizona.

Mallory himself garnered some fame when he left Tybee to attend the University of Georgia and Chicago University.

At Georgia, he studied under Eugene Odum in the Institute of Ecology. Odum is widely known as the "father of ecology," and it was through working with him, along with Mallory's early interest in birds and marshes on Tybee, that he developed his life-long affinity for the preservation of nature.

After majoring in zoology at Chicago and briefly returning to Tybee, Mallory headed to California where he obtained a Master of Fine Arts degree from UCLA. While there he studied animation under Jay Ward, creator of *Rocky and Bullwinkle.*

For his thesis at UCLA, Mallory produced a short film entitled *DNA, A Blueprint for Life* in 1968, a film still widely used in classrooms around the country. He also worked with a number of Disney Studio filmmakers and produced another notable short film, *Printing, Plain and Fancy*, a history of the evolution of writing styles beginning with the Romans. That film, narrated by John Houseman and acquired by Disney, is still shown occasionally on the Disney Channel.

Mallory checks out bird in his back yard.

Mallory is joined in his Tybee yard by fellow city council candidates, left to right, Anne Monaghan, Pam O'Brien and Shirley Sessions.

And don't be fooled by Mallory's seeming omnipresence on the beach bar scene. Since returning to Tybee, he's been busy teaching art and calligraphy at Armstrong College mornings and film history evenings at St. Leo's on Hunter Air Force Base.

He also says he makes it a point to stop by City Hall daily to confer with the city manager and check on matters relating to ecology.

Mallory campaigned for his council seat on a platform stressing ecological preservation. He was elected last November, garnering one of the top vote tallies.

Since his return to Tybee he has also established the

Tybee Environmental Committee and is a volunteer member of the Georgia Natural Resource Committee.

One of his major current interests is the Tybee Island Land Trust which he helped establish and now heads. Its purpose is to encourage property owners to set aside land for the preservation of nature, particularly in the areas that border marshes and maritime forests.

Mainly, Mallory says, he wants to preserve the quality of life on Tybee and ensure that its natural resources are not overextended.

He says island residents are comprised of "the rich and not so wealthy at Tybee, and all of them come to places like the DeSoto to drink beer together, and that's part of the quality of life too."

To this end, Mallory is constantly doing his part, brew in hand.

POSTSCRIPT: Mallory Pearce has become a well-known calligraphist and artist and has written and illustrated books about the ecology of coastal Georgia and the Low Country of South Carolina. Now 88, he is hard at work on his autobiography, while occasionally still slipping out to sip a brew at one of Tybee's many bistros.

Kathryn Williams - Community Service Runs in Her Family

Spreading Joy Beside The Beach

Teaching, public service and political action are the anchors of Kathryn Williams' life...outside her husband and family.

You can hear the joy in her voice as she retrieves a live horseshoe crab from a tank at Tybee's Marine Science Center and describes it to a group of wide-eyed children.

Spurred by her audience's enthusiasm, Kathryn's own eyes seem to sparkle as she tickles the crab's wriggling legs and rubs its belly while describing its habitat and characteristics.

The kids giggle, then step back a bit when she tells them the prehistoric looking creature is not a crab at all but an arachnid (a member of the spider family). They are spellbound by Kathryn's effervescent presentation.

This kind of learning is fun for a six-year-old. Kathryn's clearly having just as much fun with the teaching.

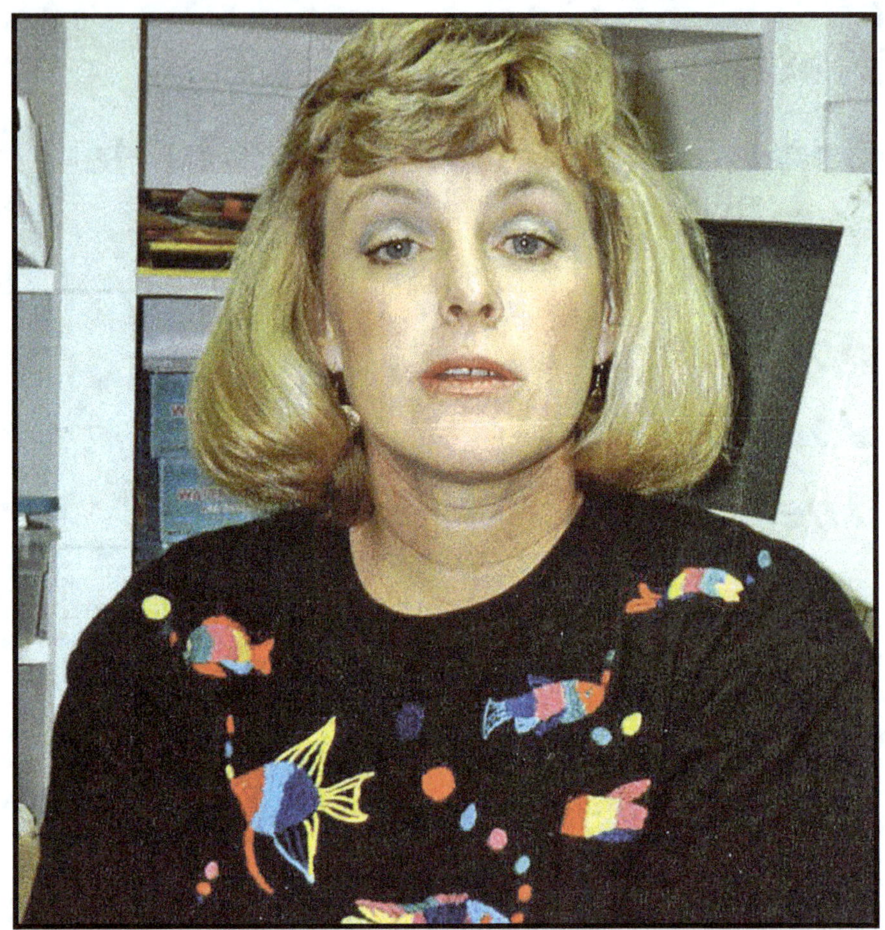

Kathryn Williams claims teaching is better than ever.

That's what she does.

She's been an elementary school teacher in the Savannah school system for almost 20 years, beginning as a student teacher while she was still an undergraduate at Armstrong State College.

And she's never lost her enthusiasm for her chosen field.

"It's better now than ever," she says. "Children today come to first grade with considerably more knowledge.

Many are reading, and a lot of them are writing. It's wonderful."

Kathryn attributes this to expanded exposure to learning, both from television and increased mobility.

Parents now take their children on vacation trips all over the country and "they take time on those trips to take their children to museums and other interesting places where they learn things," she says.

Kathryn also believes there is a growing stability in home life, with more children living with "their biological parents" and those parents helping more with the learning process.

She says the downside of exposure to television is there is too much of it, and it carries inappropriate subject matter.

"Sometimes, when you turn the television on, there will be a frightening scene of fighting somewhere, and the children will see it and absorb it before you can change the station," she says.

And the pace of the programs is so fast that kids get used to it and this sometimes results in their finding regular school classes "boring because they don't move at that speed."

Kathryn tries to reduce the impact of television on her own children by limiting their viewing to a half hour a day and making sure that after school, in addition to their music lessons and homework, they get outside to play.

"They need to be outside playing with their friends and

getting exercise," she says.

She believes the school system itself has also improved in recent years.

"The overall school administration and the new site-based management, where teachers have a lot more power in decision making" are among the biggest improvements from her initial teaching days, she says.

While Kathryn was born and raised in Savannah, where her parents, grandparents, and great grandparents (the latter immigrating from Europe) lived, "Tybee was always the highlight of the week, coming out to the beach on weekends," she says.

"When I was a teenager, I'd do anything to get car privileges to get out to the beach. I'd shell butterbeans and do all sorts of little jobs to earn the use of the car."

Her husband, Stephen, was a resident of Tybee, but they met on River Street in Savannah while they were there "on an outing" with their two separate groups.

They married while still in college and moved to Tybee 17 years ago.

Stephen and Kathryn now have two sons, 11 and 12, who she says are "Tybee boys through and through. They're up in the morning, swimming in the Back River or at the beach. They just love it."

Kathryn says she inherited her penchant for community service from her family, noting: "Volunteerism runs in my family. My Mom was very involved in the Humane Society and her church, and my grandmother was always volunteering at the Thunderbolt Library. My mother-in-law has worked since her retirement at the Tybee Light.

"I just think there are so many personal benefits that come from being involved from things like this that we love it."

In addition to her activities at the Marine Science Center, of which she is president, Kathryn works with the Tybee Beautification Association and the Tybee Environmental Committee.

She's worked with the beautification group, which improves city signs, plants trees, and improves city parks and median strips, for about ten years.

The group also organizes a twice a year Beach Sweep.

The most recent one, held in September, found hundreds of people involved in the cleanup, circling the island, mostly on their hands and knees, picking up cigarette butts and other assorted trash.

Kathryn first became concerned with keeping the beaches clean when she brought her sons down to swim.

"I'd be cleaning up the trash while they swam. Finally, I went down to City Hall to complain about the trash, and Mayor Parker put me on a Litter Committee."

She has been active politically and in protecting the environment ever since.

"We've just got to protect our green space," she says. "I'm concerned about our environment. I don't want it to control us, but we have to protect it."

And you'll see her at virtually every monthly city council meeting, actively and vocally weighing in on the many issues which interest her.

One of her biggest concerns recently is the city's building height restriction, currently a volatile topic on Tybee.

But her real love, and the one that takes most of her time and energy, seems to be the Marine Science Center.

The center opened in 1988 in a former beachside police station at the foot of Tybrisa Street.

The center, initially functioning only during the summer, is now open year round and has substantially expanded its exhibits and programs.

It now features a shark tank and tanks containing local and tropical fish, along with special rooms displaying fossilized whale bones, sharks' teeth, and educational material about the sea and shore.

It also has a gift shop, a "touch tank," classrooms, and office space.

The shark and touch tanks, the latter containing a wide variety of shells, plants, and sea creatures, are by far the most popular exhibits, particularly with children.

Much of the equipment and many of the items on display were donated by individuals and groups who contribute to the museum.

The center also sponsors fundraisers to help finance its

operation, although basic operational funding is provided by the city.

Members of the center's staff now conduct field trips frequently for various groups.

The trips include walks around the island inspecting flora and fauna, sifting the sand to discover small creatures and elements, and using a seine net to catch and discuss surf fish.

Lectures on the geology of the beach are included, along with microscope viewing in the center, which also features a small wave making machine.

The trips are particularly popular with the growing number of Girl Scouts who visit the area in the summer and with elementary classes when schools are in session.

"It's a wonderful hands-on education," says Kathryn.

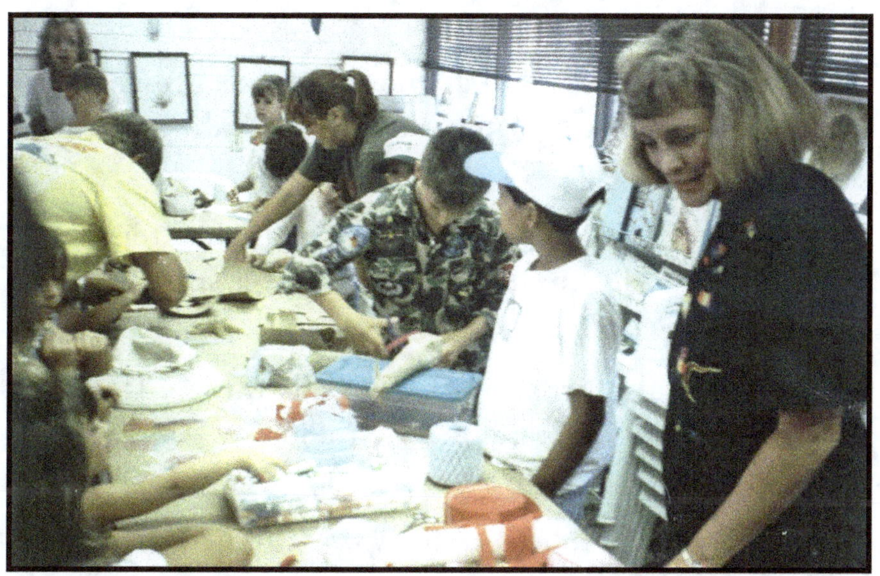

Kathryn, right, discusses marine life with kids.

"The kids just love it."

Proof of this was graphically illustrated recently when a group of school children attended the center's Peanut Butter and Jellyfish program, one of its annual year-end sessions.

They laughed and learned as they listened to lectures on sea life while constructing jellyfish from bubble plastic packing material and tissue streamers, puffer fish from paper bags and toothpicks, and sea stars from brown paper.

Kathryn joined other staffers in assisting the enthusiastic children.

Older visitors take delight in the center's Moon Walk field trips on the beach at night.

They observe such things as the water's phosphorescence and have participated in counting turtles when they're hatching.

Interest in and visitation at the center has grown substantially since the new pavilion opened adjacent to it this summer.

"A lot of people who were unaware of the center now come down to the pavilion, see the center, and come in," Kathryn says.

The pavilion also brought another advantage. It provided the center with a pipe line to deliver sea water for its aquariums.

"We used to have to carry the water from the beach in buckets," says Kathryn.

The staff includes a salaried director and several part-time staff workers. A number of volunteers also assist in its operation.

Kathryn says the center hopes to further expand its activities in the future if funds are available.

Among other things, they would like to build a deck on the roof and install telescopes to view the island and surrounding area, along with the stars at night.

Expansion of the center's space in the building, which also houses the lifeguard station and public restrooms, is another dream, says Kathryn.

And you can count on her being there to help push such plans along. Kathryn says she'll remain in her position "until they get tired of me" or "somebody else wants the job."

Given the extraordinary time and effort she expends in the position and the increasing success of the center's operation under her auspices, there appears to be little danger of this.

POSTSCRIPT: Kathryn Williams became even more active in community affairs, running for and being elected to City Council. She more than exceeded those dreams of expanding her beloved Marine Science Center when she spearheaded the successful drive to build the new, far larger and more impressive center on the north end of the island. In addition, she became part owner of the popular North Beach Grill which she managed

until her retirement in 2022. You can find her these days attending numerous city government meetings and reporting on them for "Forever Tybee," a group devoted to positive activisim and informing the public about important issues on Tybee.

Mike Scarbrough -

Chasing Dolphins and the Good Life

Tybee Tour Guide Gains National Recognition

Most people know him simply as "Capt. Mike," proprietor of a phenomenally popular dolphin tour business on Tybee Island.

Mike Scarbrough started his tours just over a decade ago using an old 26-foot boat he spotted in a junkyard beside Louisville Road in Savannah.

He rebuilt the engine, named the former military utility craft "S.S. Dolphin," and erected a frame above the open passenger area on which he strung palm fronds to protect customers from the elements.

It took a while for his business to thrive.

On some days he headed out with only two passengers, and during his first year's operation, when he and daughter Lisa, then 16, worked the boat alone, they had only about 1,000 customers.

Since that time, the business has mushroomed, and Mike has become a familiar figure to people all across the country.

Capt. Mike, who many call the king of dolphin tour operators along the entire East Coast, has a fleet of seven tour boats, two of them 50-feet-long and capable of carrying 49 passengers each.

The gregarious captain gained wide recognition when his dolphin excursions were featured on national television in the 1990s.

The tours "really took off when we were on Good Morning America," he says, laughing as he remembers the show's then weatherman, Spencer Christian, "just went nuts over the dolphins coming up to the boat."

Mike Scarbrough at the helm of one of his dolphin tour boats passing Cockspur Light.

"I told him it doesn't seem like it takes much to entertain you fellas from New York."

"The program wasn't over five minutes before the phone started ringing. I mean we got calls from everywhere."

Customers sometimes travel long distances to take his tours and he is especially pleased that many of them are youngsters.

Mike says children are the real reason he started the business.

"When they closed the water slide, there was nothing for children to do and I wanted to start a business" catering to kids, he says. "Since Savannah is the home of the Girl Scouts, I wanted to target them and we went after that market."

Mike and his wife, Iris, attended national Girl Scout conventions in Kansas and California to spread the word about their tours. They also became members of the Scout's Circle of Friends, contributing to the renovation of the Juliette Gordon Low Birthplace.

"Every year we give a substantial donation," says Mike, who admits the money comes back many-fold through the hundreds of scouting groups taking his tours.

Mike spends considerable time helping children in other ways as well.

Two years ago, Chatham County honored him with its Citizen of the Year Award for the free dolphin trips he gave to hundreds of inner city children.

Mike, a former president of the Tybee Light Shrine Club, says he spends "a lot of time with the Shrine because that's working with children."

"There's usually 25 to 30 kids from this area that we send to the Shrine hospital every year."

"Everybody remembers what they were doing on 9/11. That's when Iris and I took a little three-and-a-half-year-old boy and his mother up to the Shrine hospital in Greenville, South Carolina."

"The boy had already had seven operations. Normally you really feel good when you do something like that because you're doing something for a kid," but his joy was diminished on this trip because of the airplane attacks.

"We were going through Columbia when the first plane crashed and that was all that was on the radio all day and on the TV at the hospital."

Mike's somber spirits were immediately raised when they arrived at the hospital, and "the little boy got up from his mother and came over and grabbed my arm and told his mother: Mike is my new best friend."

He also recalls when a young boy from Rincon was shot a while back and local doctors told the family he would likely "be paralyzed for the rest of his life."

"The Shriners down here put together $25,000 to hire a plane and take him to the Shrine hospital" and the boy's chances for recovery are now considered good.

Mike also helped fulfill one of the last wishes of a nine-year-old boy from Cincinnati, through the Make a Wish

Foundation last year.

"He was interested in marine life and birds and the Make a Wish people just called explaining they were going to send him to Hawaii but they didn't have time. I guess he was in the process of dying."

Mike took the boy and his parents out deep-sea fishing as part of a round of activities on Tybee that included a stay at the DeSoto Beach Hotel and a party at the Crab Shack.

He says the boy's biggest thrill came when Tybee Police Cpl. Jason Heckman picked him up at the DeSoto and drove him to the Crab Shack in his police car with its blue lights flashing and siren screaming.

"That just thrilled him," says Mike, who was driving behind Heckman's car and claims "it's lot better than being in front of one."

Mike has gained a reputation for performing other community services as well.

When the summer Olympics sailing events were staged off Tybee, he provided space on his property for any participant who needed a place to camp.

"We had the U.S. team here and they would fish in the evening and we'd do a low country boil," he recalls. "They'd bring their guitars and sit out on the dock and play and sing."

Judging from the number of cats, dogs and birds meandering in and out of his house, Mike has an affinity for all animals, but he's developed a special relationship with dolphins over the years.

Not long ago he headed up a dangerous expedition to save one from almost certain death.

He heard a call to the Coast Guard over his marine radio saying a large dolphin was tangled in a crab trap in the Savannah River channel.

When the Coast Guard referred the call to Coastal Resources in Brunswick, Mike realized that by the time a crew could arrive from that far away it would be too late, so he took matters into his own hands.

He called Weeks Dredging Project Manager Mike Ward, who was working nearby, and persuaded him and a co-worker to join him in a rescue attempt.

A swift incoming tide made their effort more difficult every minute, but luck was with the trio.

They spotted the dolphin with a rope wrapped around its body, struggling to reach the surface for air.

Mike thinks the dolphin got tied up in the line from a crab trap when the trap was still in about 15 feet of water and dragged it out into the deep channel.

"It was exhausted," he says. "It could barely stick its head above the surface to take a breath when we got there."

"I reached down and grabbed the dolphin's tail after we dragged the tangle of lines and trap to the boat. A dolphin that size could pull the entire boat but this one was so weak it couldn't pull away from me."

"I held its tail while the others got down and cut the rope with a knife. You could see where the line had dug into the dolphin's skin."

Mike sips a beverage at Tybee Lighthouse reception.

While the rescue effort was underway a large ship headed towards the group in the channel, placing it directly in harm's way, but they refused to abandon their mission.

Disaster was averted when Mike was able to raise the Coast Guard by radio and have it alert the approaching ship.

Once released, the dolphin floated on its side while the rescuers stayed with it for almost an hour, hoping for the best. Eventually, it started floating upright, then went under for a couple of seconds and back up.

The dolphin continued this motion, extending the time with each repetition until it finally made a normal dive before returning to the surface.

"On the last dive we thought the dolphin had recovered and left, but it came up behind the boat where we were as if to say thanks before swimming off into the fog," says Mike.

"The three of us stood there looking at each other, not saying a thing."

In addition to his leadership in the Shrine club, Mike has served as a Trustee of the Tybee Island Marine Science Foundation that supports the Center, two terms as president of the Chamber of Commerce, and three terms as president of Tybee Beautification Association.

He says his move to the island and the creation of the dolphin tour were somewhat serendipitous.

Mike, Iris and Lisa had been driving to Tybee from Atlanta every weekend for almost five years to relax on a boat they kept near the Crab Shack on Chimney Creek.

"Every Friday afternoon at 5:30 we left Atlanta, drove to Tybee, and went back on Sunday night," he says.

While crossing the Lazaretto Creek Bridge on the way back to Atlanta one Sunday evening, Mike spotted a little shack by a dilapidated dock on the creek below.

Intrigued, he swung his car around, drove down and knocked on the door of the shack he says belonged to W.G. Smith, who operated two shrimp boats from the site.

"I asked him if he would sell it and he said well, you know, anything is for sale," according to Mike. "I sat there and talked to him and before we left to go to Atlanta, I gave him a deposit on the property."

"About two weeks later he wanted out" but Mike says he wrote the property's PIN number and "deposit for" on his check and the former owner cashed it so "it was like a contract."

"I told him, well, I figure I can turn around and sell that property and make about $200,000. You give me my check back and $200,000 and you won't have to speak to my attorney."

The deal went through after that conversation, according to Mike, who says the two have subsequently become friends.

Smith still keeps a shrimp boat on the creek and his son plans to work as a captain on one of Mike's dolphin boats this summer.

Prior to his move to Tybee, Mike was employed in the construction business for 23 years.

Among his projects, he built something like 30 Days Inns, shortly after Cecil Day created the first motel of his popular chain on Tybee.

While working in Atlanta, Mike lived aboard a 37-foot cruiser on Lake Altoona for a while. That's where he met Iris. Both were divorced parents at the time. Mike had two girls, Iris a boy.

"I guess she wasn't used to being around somebody that drank that much because after a while she said she was gonna go home," Mike recalls. "I said I'll take you and she said no, you've had too much to drink."

"About three weeks later I decided, what the hell, and called her. I had my girls and she had her son and we went rafting down the Chattahoochee."

"Iris and I were in one raft and we had the kids in the raft behind us. It started pouring down rain and the kids dumped my beer out and put the cooler over their heads!"

That must have been a magic moment, since they married immediately after that excursion and Iris later gave birth to Lisa. They've now been married for 31 years and still seem very much in love.

Mike first discovered Tybee while overseeing the construction of several Burger Kings in Savannah and was instantly smitten. Iris was equally attracted when he brought her down, which led to all those visits from Atlanta.

After acquiring the Lazaretto property, Mike retired from his construction business and lived on his boat on the creek while rebuilding the docks.

"Iris kept her job in Atlanta for a while because we did

have to eat," he says.

While installing the marina's docks, Mike also refurbished a one-bedroom house on the property, adding a deck and new pilings for support and tearing out all the walls.

"Then I built a bar in there and opened up," he says.

Mike operated the bar until his friend Elton moved down from Atlanta to help run the place.

He says Elton, who still works with him at the marina, kept a cot in the bar and when he was ready to go to sleep, he unfolded it "and then everybody had to wait on themselves. The last person out at night had to lock the door."

"Iris says she doesn't know if we made any money but everybody had a good time. People just wandered down. It didn't even have a name. People just called it Mike's place."

"It's where all the bikers and commercial fishermen came to drink beer. They'd go down to 16th Street and start drinking at the Anchor Bar and call me about 5 o'clock and I'd go down there and get them. They'd drink at my place until midnight."

Mike says the bikers never caused him a problem but Ray McMillan, then owner of the Anchor, complained that they frequently wrecked his place during fights, and wondered why the same crowd acted differently at Mike's.

"I told him, you know, these guys are basically good. If you tell them what the rules are, they'll follow 'em.

Your problem is you don't have any rules."

One of Mike's rules was that no profanity could be used because Iris and Lisa did their cooking in the back kitchen while they lived on the boat.

"A guy came in one time and started cussing and I told him I didn't have any of that in here and if you want to stay and drink, you're going to have to watch your mouth," says Mike.

"Then he started again, and I said you have to get out and he said something else and I started around the bar. When I started toward him two bikers grabbed him and threw him out in the parking lot, I mean like a Frisbee!"

Mike and Iris eventually moved off their boat and into an old house they refurbished at the marina for use as both their home and office.

The house was built in 1887 and was originally occupied by the bridge tender who operated the old railroad bridge across Lazaretto Creek. The train tracks ran right beside the house.

Their home is adjacent to the structure Mike converted into a bar, which has been transformed into the popular Café Loco, now operated by Joel Solomon.

Despite their financial success, Iris still spends long hours handling the dolphin tour's office work while Mike labors around the marina on most days from daylight until well after dark. You can often find him in grease up to his elbows working on an engine on one of his boats.

Mike Scarbrough, left, looks on as Joel Solomon, right, operator of the Cafe Loco on Lazeretto Creek, presents Cullen Chambers a fund raising check.

Given the spectacular appreciation in the value of their waterfront property, Mike and Iris could easily bail out and live very comfortably for the rest of their lives anywhere they care to go.

"But I can't think of any place I'd rather be than here," says Mike, looking out over the miles of unspoiled marsh on the far side of the creek behind his house. "That's why I haven't given any thought to selling this place."

"I've got six grandsons and every summer they'll come down and stay with me for a couple of weeks. That's why it's worth keeping this property."

"They come down here and they talk to the fishermen and shrimpers and they know all about the life cycle of the shrimp and all about manatees and dolphins."

Listening to Mike, it's hard not to agree that this is about as good as it gets.

POSTSCRIPT: Iris Hembree Scarbrough was 72 when she passed away on Dec. 3, 2019. Capt. Mike's health deteriorated after losing his wife of 45 years. He passed away at 75, on March 4, 2021.

Charlie Sherrill -

He's Done It...

Just Like He Said He Would

Tybee's popular Pied Piper has just completed an album, the culmination of almost two years' work.

The album, entitled *Palm Street*, includes a dozen of Charlie Sherrill's original tunes featuring Charlie on his assortment of saxophones and a flute.

Primarily instrumental, it includes two tunes with vocals, Can You Tell Me and Dreaming. The former is a favorite among the clientele at Doc's Bar, where Charlie has held forth as the house musician for two years now. He also performs with Playing for Keeps, a blues band that plays throughout the area.

Although he had initially planned to record all instrumentals, "I had to include *Can You Tell Me*," he says. "Everyone wanted and expected it."

Having included it, Charlie says he was compelled to include *Dreaming* on the flip side for balance.

For my money, *Whitney's Theme*, the second cut on side

one, is the piece de resistance. It's light as a summer breeze and will have you swaying like a willow within the first few bars.

The entire grouping mellows you out like a snooze in a hammock.

All of the tunes will be familiar to habitues of Doc's Bar late evenings on Wednesdays and weekends when Charlie's on stage since he selected those which have been audience favorites.

He had a large selection to choose from. Charlie has a band box full of original songs.

Charlie Sherrill at home at Doc's Bar.

And he not only wrote and performed the songs on the recording but did all the production work himself in his island studio, which is stocked with the latest in multi-track, digital recording equipment.

The clean quality of his CD has already attracted a number of area musicians.

Charlie is now working with Rick and Debbie Sheridan, the regular performers at the DeSoto Beach Hotel, on the production of an album for them.

That's an area in which he hopes to become more active in the future, and he's well equipped to do it, not only with his constantly upgraded studio but his extensive training in engineering for recording.

A graduate of Berklee School of Music in Boston who's been working as a professional musician for 30 years, Charlie was trained in engineering at Criteria Studios in Miami. That was the home studio for the BeeGees, and James Brown recorded there in his early days.

It was there, as well, that Eric Clapton met Duane Allman of the Allman Brothers. Following that meeting the two did all the guitar work for Derek and the Dominoes' *LayLa* album, which became a classic.

Charlie wound up playing with a band while taking engineering classes at Criteria, honing his own skills during repeated training sessions.

He also spent time in a studio in Muscle Shoals, Alabama, which many consider the popular music capitol of the world, working with Barry Beckett who was a producer for The Rolling Stones, Gladys Knight, and Linda Ronstadt, among others.

Charlie performs with his friend Conga Dave.

Charlie played for a number of years with the Truly Dangerous Swamp Band and Cameron, while both bands performed at colleges and dance halls throughout the eastern United States, before he broke free and headed to Tybee to be on his own, play his own material and showcase his extraordinary talent on the sax and flute.

"Playing with rock-based bands you'd only get maybe two 30-second solos on the flute in a night," he said. "I've really been able to experiment and develop my technique in my present setup. I can try things out on the audience and find out what works and what doesn't."

Charlie's new recording has drawn the attention of several radio stations which plan to give him air time and he has received feelers from a couple of big-name recording studios.

"But you have to be careful," he says. "You have to have the right deal. It's the quality of the deal that counts. You have to know someone has the commitment and will put forth the effort and money to promote your work."

Charlie learned about that with Cameron. That band had a recording contract with a name studio and, while they produced an album, it never saw the light of day.

Based on the success of his current recording ("It's selling better than I ever expected," he says), Charlie is already at work on a second one, which will include more vocals.

He may also do some live recording at Doc's Bar, and he's rolling all the profit from his current album into the latest sound equipment for his studio.

If things fall into place with a recording contract and

Charlie plays at Tybee art studio.

Charlie and Doc's Bar owner Wanda Parker.

exposure on national radio Charlie says he might even organize another band, but it would have to be a big production, concert-type operation to get him back out on the road.

"I did that one-night stand touring thing for years and I'm not going to get back into that," he vows.

Meanwhile, islanders are the winners with Charlie's talent still on display, live and in person, at Tybee Island's popular Doc's Bar.

POSTSCRIPT: Charlie Sherrill recorded several additional albums following the success of the first. One of those includes a tune called "Highway 80" about ending life's journey on Tybee Island, written by yours truly. Charlie continued playing at area venues until the virtual shutdown of large entertainment gatherings by the Covid epidemic in early 2020. In August of that year he moved to Virginia to become the principal caregiver for his mother, following her major back surgery. He remained with her until she passed away on March 27, 2023. Charlie says he hopes to return to his music career at some point in the future but for now "I am still getting over the passing of my mother."

Marie Rodriguez -

Pet Lover Running a Mile a Minute

Marie Rodriguez

Entrepreneur Keeps Her Plate Full

Marie Rodriguez is an overcomer and a whirlwind, a regular whirling dervish rushing about the islands bent on giving something back to the community while carrying out a basketful of jobs to achieve economic independence.

Just hearing about her interests is exhausting. Marie rattles off her activities like a machine gun firing an inexhaustible supply of ammunition.

She heads a pet sitting business; her own version of the Welcome Wagon; keeps accounts and works as a receptionist for a veterinarian; handles advertising sales and serves as a representative for a student exchange program.

Marie is also active in the church, heads the membership committee for the Wilmington Island Optimist Club, and is program chairman for the Tybee Arts Association.

A Tybee resident for the last eight years, she was born

in Miami, where she says her parents "met on a street corner."

Her mother, Mimi, emigrated to Miami from Havana before the Castro fiasco. Her father, Frank, originally from Warrenville, South Carolina ("It's so small that even if you're looking for the sign, you'll drive right past it," she laughs), was stationed with the U.S. Coast Guard in Miami when they met.

While fortuitous, her parents' street-corner meeting was not what it might seem at first, based on Marie's bemused description.

Both were accompanied by several friends when the Coast Guardsmen casually asked the group of girls if they would join his group at a nearby dance hall.

Mimi says her grandfather was a colonel in the Cuban Liberation Army, and her grandmother was a spy during the Spanish American War.

"We come from a long line of strong women," she says proudly.

Marie claims her great-grandmother was almost caught on a clandestine mission but managed to hide the intelligence material she was carrying under her dress "and no man in those days was going to look under a woman's dress."

Her grandfather was a veterinarian in Cuba but had to regain his vet's license the hard way after moving to Miami, starting from scratch by cleaning out dog kennels and working his way up to technician, before finally obtaining his doctor's credentials once more.

Following his retirement from the Coast Guard, her father moved to Washington, where he handled framing and the restoration of paintings for the White House.

He met several presidents during his employment in the White House and introduced Marie to President Reagan in 1986.

Marie spent her school years in Tampa, where her father was stationed following his Coast Guard tour in Miami.

Shortly after completing high school she met and married Julio, a U.S. Marine. They moved to Beaufort, South Carolina when her husband was transferred to Parris Island.

Marie wanted to improve their economic situation by getting a job, but claims Julio was dead set against it.

After endless conversations, she finally persuaded him to let her apply for a position as a receptionist for the Bremer Veterinary Clinic in Beaufort. Because of her previous experience helping her grandfather in Tampa and her natural love of animals, this figured to be an ideal spot for her.

After she learned that 97 people had applied for the same job, Marie was sure her odds of landing it were nil.

She was dismayed, while Julio felt a bit better. Both of their emotions proved to be momentary because "miracle of all miracles, I got the job," says Marie.

She says Julio "was kinda mad, but he knew if I got it when they had 97 candidates, they must have wanted

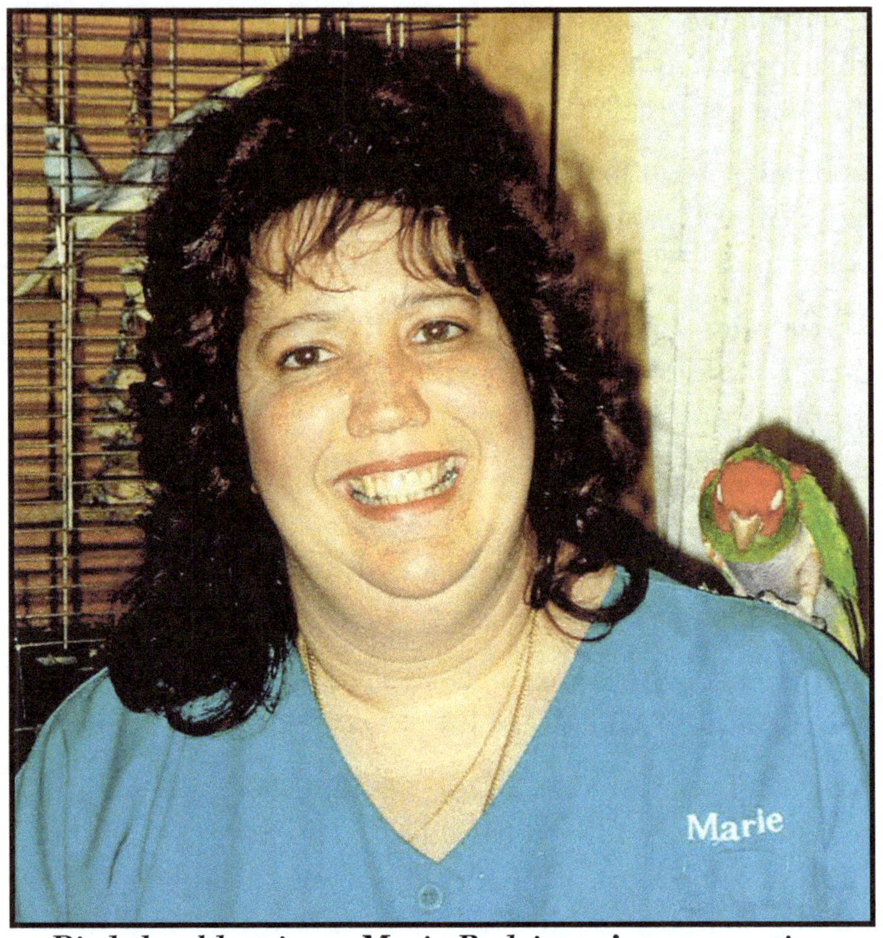

Bird shoulders in on Marie Rodriguez's conversation.

me, so he let me do it."

During her employment at the clinic, Marie developed a strong friendship with Dr. Bremer and his wife but, eventually her job, and her 5-year marriage went south when Bremer moved his clinic to Wilmington Island and Marie got a divorce.

Then she slipped south as well, heading back to her family in Tampa.

Reflecting on the demise of her marriage, Marie says it

was doomed from the start because she was too young to get married.

"Don't get married when you're 19," she advises.

Although the Bremers urged her to move to Wilmington and work with them in their new clinic, Marie says she turned the offer down "because I had been to Wilmington and Tybee, and they were just too slow."

While she preferred Tybee, where she had occasionally visited and enjoyed the beach, "it's a small place where there is nothing going on, and I was used to the big city," she says.

Her brother was a member of the Tampa Police Department, which prompted Marie, now a single mother with a young daughter to support, to take a shot at becoming a cop.

She started with a bang, making the highest grade of anyone in her group on the entry test.

Marie was the only female among those attempting to join the force at that time.

While enrolled in training classes, she decided to ride along with regular policemen to learn more about the work she would be doing, and quickly gained first-hand experience in the dangers of police work.

She found herself in the middle of a riot when the regular officer, who was driving, stopped at the edge of a milling crowd where he and his partner got out to investigate.

The squad car was suddenly surrounded by a mob

which formed after a drug deal went bad and, unable to escape, she scrunched down in the back seat while the angry crowd turned several cars over.

Marie says she was convinced hers would be next to go because "the officer was armed with only a shotgun, and I knew he couldn't get too many shots off if the crowd didn't back down. It was pretty scary."

She breathed a sigh of relief when another police car pulled up and the crowd dispersed.

"I figured OK, that wasn't too bad, I can deal with that," she recalls.

On another occasion, the officer with whom she was riding responded to a call about a body in a dumpster.

When they arrived at the scene, a puddle of blood had formed at the base of the dumpster and Marie watched in horror as the officer climbed into the trash bin to check it out.

The "body" turned out to be a four-foot-long slab of beef someone had dumped.

"Well, this is still not too bad," she recalls thinking at the time.

The trauma of her police work was often interspersed with less serious moments.

She accompanied the undercover narcotics team on a stakeout at a Seven-Eleven store where one of the team members crawled stealthily into undergrowth near the store. He was to remain quiet and whisper into his twoway radio to alert his cohorts who were waiting in nearby cars when he spotted a deal going down.

Suddenly he broke his cover, shouting deafening obscenities while his partners braced for a disaster.

They were relieved, while he was obviously not, when they discovered he had crawled atop a nest of fire ants.

"He was very unhappy about that," she recalls.

It was while on another narcotics mission that she changed her mind about police work.

They were staking out a house where a suspected crack cocaine dealer was reported to be holed up, and the team slipped through the fence surrounding the place and kicked down the front door "just like you see on TV," she says.

When Marie approached the same fence while attempting to follow the team, a snarling pit bulldog charged, apparently aiming to make her his next meal.

"He just ignored the others and came at me, and I screamed for them to shoot him if he got me because he would have killed me," she shudders.

The fence stopped the dog, but even though he failed to bite her, the experience left an indelible impression.

Not only did she cop out on cop work, she learned pit bulls were not her pet of preference.

"Once I got involved with the police department and saw how much crime was going on in the big city, I wanted out," she says. "There's just too much crime. It's a day-to-day battle fighting drugs, and it's no place to raise your child."

Those "too slow" islands to the north were beginning to look a lot more attractive, and Marie called the Bremers to determine if their offer was still open.

After finding it was, and that they promised to put her up in their home until she found a place to live, she packed up and headed for Wilmington Island in 1991.

Marie quickly became reacquainted with Tybee and, after the trauma of Tampa, discovered she loved the place and was particularly attracted to the relaxing atmosphere and friendly residents.

"You get to know everybody very quickly," she says. "Everybody was so nice and polite and helpful to me, and I knew that this was the place I wanted to raise my child."

Unlike some laid back islanders, however, Marie hit the ground running and hasn't stopped since.

"It's important to me for people to see just how far I have come," she says. "You just work at it. Here I was, a divorced mother with a 4-year-old, never having had but one job, so I had no skills whatsoever, and I moved here and started to work for the clinic."

After working with the Bremers for a while, Marie decided she needed a job with fringe benefits and became employed as a clerk with the Magistrate's Court in Savannah, while still serving as accounts manager for the clinic.

To earn additional money, she took a job as office manager for a computer company in Savannah, only to be laid off during a staff reduction in December of 1997.

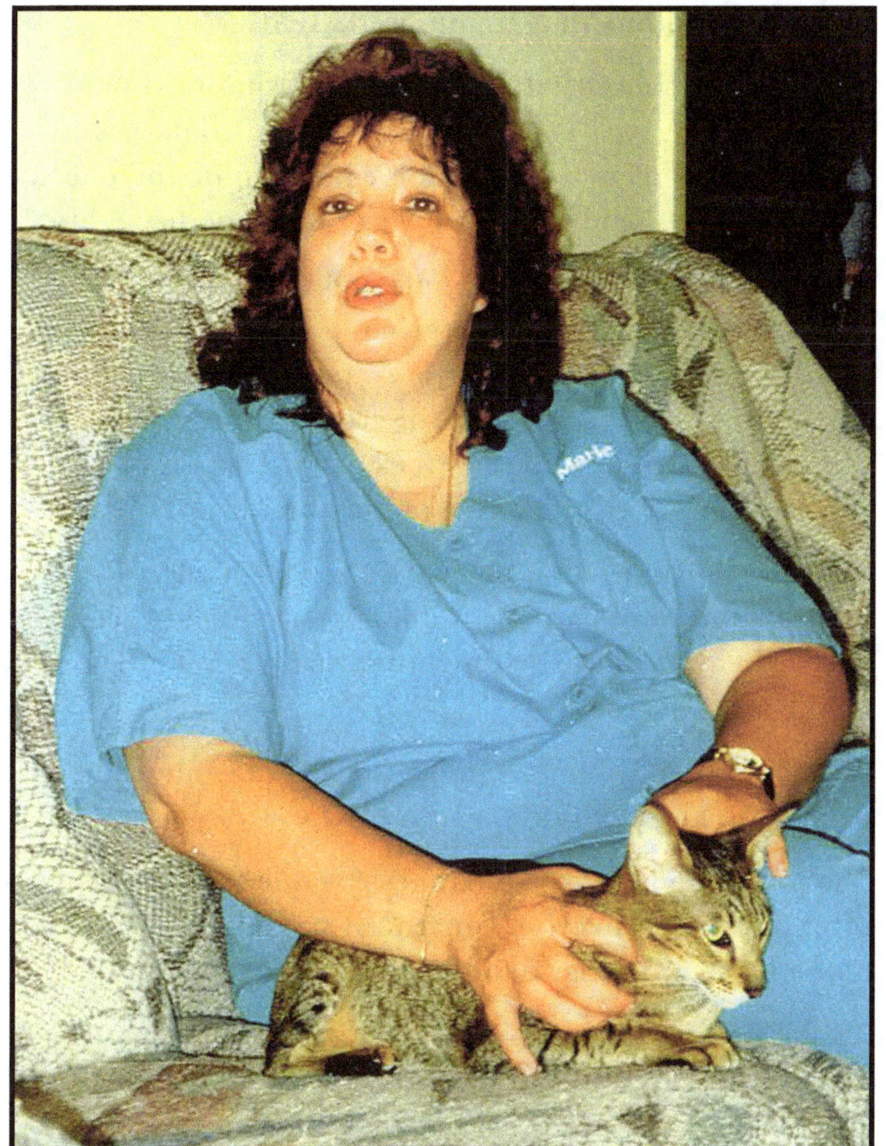

Marie takes a break at home with one of her cats.

That's when Marie turned entrepreneur, opening her own pet sitting business, "Islands Critter Sitters."

"A lot of people don't want their pets to be boarded since pets hate change from the environment, so I decided to build up this business," she says. "I have the time to spend morning, noon, and night."

"I think the thing that separates me from most people in this business is that I go to people's houses and spend a lot of time there. I don't just run in and check their litter box and food and water and run out again.

"I spend time with the animals and make sure they're OK, and I have 13 years veterinary experience, so I can tell if an animal is dehydrated or not eating or drinking correctly or has worms in their stools, things that the owner or someone who just does pet sitting on the side because they need the extra money might not notice."

She also continues to work with the veterinary clinic handling accounts and occasionally serving as receptionist in addition to selling advertising for the Island's telephone directory.

"I'm a good salesman because I only sell something I believe in, and I would never lie," she says.

She purchased a house on Jones Avenue four years ago after a quick inspection convinced her it was the ideal home for her and her daughter, Marie, who is now 14.

"But they were asking $139,900, and I knew I couldn't afford that so I just sat down and prayed about it," she says, adding that her prayers were answered when the owner accepted her offer of $85,500.

"I've come from being a single mom with a 4-year-old child not knowing where I was going to go or what I was going to do to the point where I have a nice house and a nice car and my own business, and my child goes to St. Vincent's" she smiles, adding "I've come a long way."

Marie says she now has 200 regular Critter Sitter customers and continues to add new ones every week.

Mimi, who recently joined her daughter on Tybee, pitches in to help out with the booming pet sitting business.

"The only trouble is that I make the animals behave, and mother spoils them to death," laughs Marie. "When I go back by the houses she has handled, the pets are all crazy again because she lets them do whatever they want, and I have to get them in line again. I'm the 'drill instructor.' That's what they call me."

But while she requires the pets in her care to adhere to their regular routine, it is clear she genuinely cares about them.

"The main problem with the business is that I get too attached to the pets," she admits. "I get terribly sad when one leaves or is given away or passes away. It's hard on me."

Marie has her own menagerie at home, including four cats, three dogs, three birds, a rabbit and a hamster, most of them given to her by customers or someone who rescued them.

She's never seen an animal she could turn away, except perhaps a foul tempered pit bull.

In her limited spare time, Marie arranges the placement of exchange students in area homes for the American Inter Cultural Student Exchange Program where she serves as the Savannah area representative

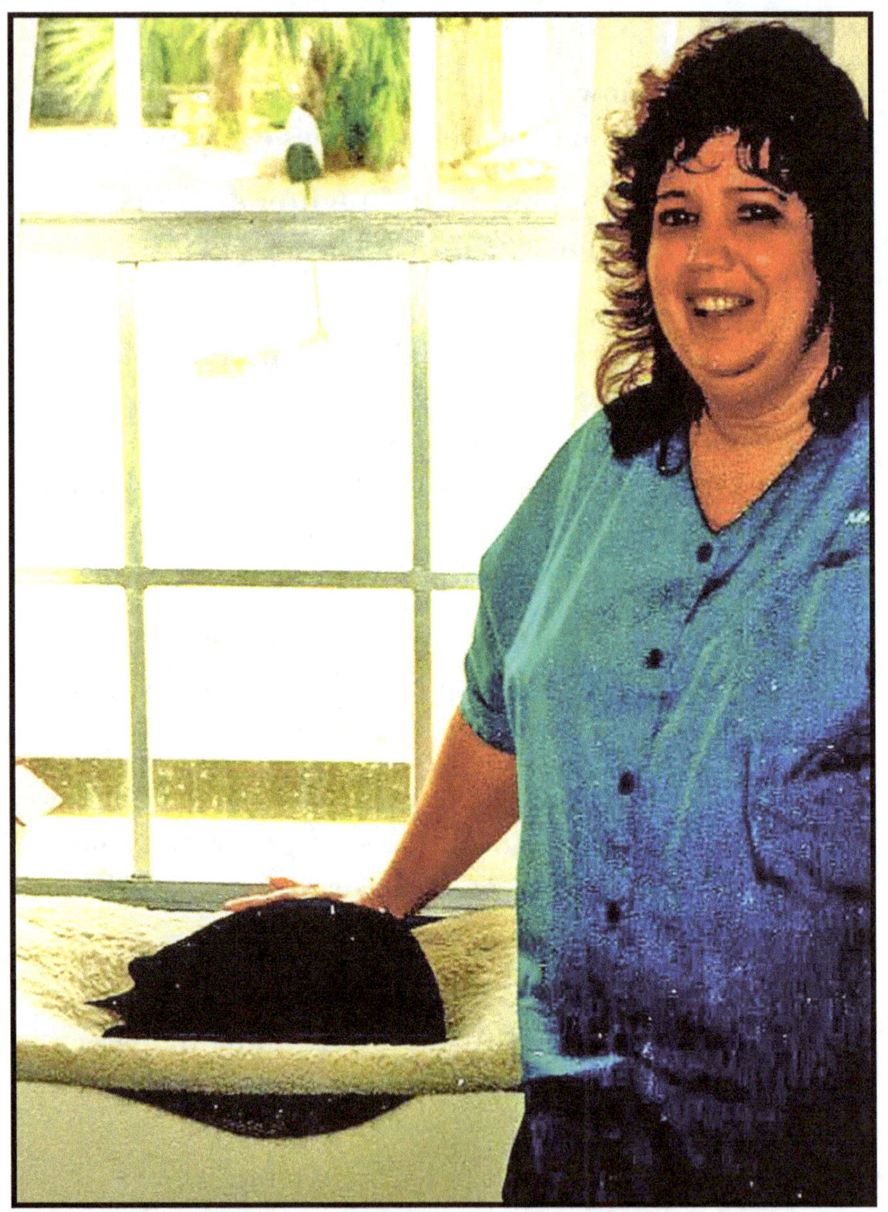

Marie gives pet cat a window seat for grooming.

while placing students as far away as St. Simons Island, Hinesville, and Sylvania.

The non-profit company matches 15- to 17-year-old

students from dozens of countries with families in the United States, generally for a semester or an entire school year.

The program is a one-way exchange, with students coming to the U.S. from overseas because "it's harder for an American student to go to a foreign country," she says.

"Their schools are a lot harder than American schools and most foreign students speak English as a second language, whereas many American students lack language skills. An American would have to speak their language and be a straight-A student just to be able to pass."

There are far more foreign students who want to come to the U.S. under this program than families volunteering to house them, and Marie says she is saddened because she must "turn away dozens of students each year. They're dying to come here."

She has developed numerous friendships through this work. The parents of her first student visitor, a German girl, even paid all the expenses for Marie and her daughter to fly to Germany to visit them.

The trip was a delightful respite from her hectic schedule, but she immediately remounted her occupational treadmill when she returned.

"When somebody asks what I do, I say I go to church, work, and home," she smiles.

That's a gross understatement, since she somehow still finds time to do volunteer work for her daughter's school, the art association, and the Optimist Club.

"I just want to give something back to the community," she smiles.

Now that her mother is here to help out, Marie says she'll have more spare time soon, especially after her ad sales for the phone directory are closed out this year.

When she does, she'll likely become involved in even more ventures.

Just thinking about it will wear you out.

POSTSCRIPT: Marie is still staying fully occupied with her many activities on the island but she somehow found time recently to run for a seat on Tybee's City Council.

Anthony Simon -

Small Man Has Big Impact on Island

Entrepreneur Sparks Business And Tourism

He's the small man with the big smile you see when you enter Cap'n Chris Restaurant on Tybee.

He'll be the one handling the cash register, greeting folks at the door, and busying himself with virtually any required chore around the place.

"I'm the adviser and the dishwasher and everything else around here," he says. "I do whatever needs to be done."

He's Anthony Simon, the man who established the business in the first place, and he's Chris' father, so what he's mostly trying to do these days is provide his son with some free labor.

But when you scratch the surface of his self-deprecating self-description, you learn that Anthony has been a hard-charging businessman and one of the island's biggest promoters for most of his life.

He brought the first national chain motel to Tybee;

operated a posh nightclub on the island; was one of the top insurance salesmen in the southeast; served as president of the island's Chamber of Commerce for three terms, during which time he initiated numerous events to boost tourism, and built a number of structures, including the new Howard Johnson's hotel on Butler Avenue.

Anthony got his start on Tybee giving tourists ocean rides aboard a surplus military amphibious craft he op-

Anthony Simon smiles while manning the cash register at son's restaurant.

erated off the beach back when he was still a teenager in the merchant marine.

He exhibited his independence earlier than that, however.

Born and reared in Savannah, he was one of seven children raised by their widowed mother, who operated a small confectionery store in the city.

Anthony left home to join the U.S. Marines when he was just 15, taking basic training at Parris Island when it was famous as a really hard-nosed boot camp.

"Hell, that was the idea in World War II," he says. "They didn't think anything about knocking you on your rear end. It wasn't one of those Hollywood versions that I went through! But I wouldn't take a million dollars for that experience."

Anthony served in the Corps for a full year before his sister revealed his age to the authorities and they reluctantly released him.

Then he joined the U.S. Merchant Marine, shipping out on vessels delivering equipment and personnel to Europe during World War II.

Anthony remembers one touchy situation he and his fellow merchant mariners found themselves in during the war.

He was aboard a hospital ship, a converted passenger liner sailing out of Charleston which was carrying a contingent of French nurses to the Riviera beachhead during the invasion of France from southern Italy.

The vessel was also carrying wounded German prisoners whose U-boat had been sunk by a U.S. destroyer that had pulled alongside the hospital ship to unload the Germans.

Anthony, still in his teens, recalls seeing one of the prisoners who was struggling along the gangplank between ships with a cast on both a leg and an arm fall in the sea and drown.

Shortly after that incident, his hospital ship found itself in the middle of harm's way, an experience that remains vivid for Anthony because he was at the helm.

"We were headed through the Straits of Messina," he says. "We were going to southern France for that invasion when we ran into a German convoy."

"I could hear the captain from my spot at the wheel saying there were ships to the port bow, ships to the starboard bow, dead astern, and all around. When the mate asked what was going on, the captain said we were in the middle of a German convoy!"

"Finally, the captain ordered us to stop all engines. Fortunately, we drifted by them, but a man on the stern said we came so close to the bow of one of the German ships that he could have jumped aboard it! That was about as close as we came to anything."

During a break in his sea service, while awaiting another ship assignment in Savannah, Anthony got a call to Tybee to handle the landing craft tour boat when the owner needed an operator with the proper seaman's certification.

"I had a ball that summer," he says. "We just had a

great time."

That memory may have helped lure him back to the beach, but before his return he ran a highly successful life insurance business in Savannah for years, starting when he was only 20.

"I lied about my age again," he laughs. "I told them I was 21."

Anthony did almost everything at a young age, including getting married.

He wed his wife, Ruth, when he was 19 (she was just 15 at the time), and they had four children, all while he was in his early 20s.

The couple have now been married for over 50 years.

Anthony took a brief break from the insurance business during the Korean Conflict when his brother, who was then a company commander with the Army Reserves, convinced him there was going to be an all-out war.

"He told me that if I joined the reserves in a transportation unit, they would be the last ones to be activated," Anthony laughs. "Forty-four days later, we were called to active duty."

Given his four dependents, he served only a year before being released to return to the insurance business. He was ultimately named southeastern director of sales for the eastern United States with 500 people reporting to him.

Anthony terminated that successful career when he says he "got tired of traveling, covering nine states,

Anthony recalls early days on Tybee.

and somehow I wound up on Tybee and got in this business."

In 1965, he purchased a rundown little bar and lounge and adjoining hotel located where the restaurant is now on Butler Avenue.

"I don't know why I did it," he says. "I hadn't given

much thought to being in that kind of business. I guess I thought I was going to work three or four months a year and go fishing the rest of the time. It didn't work out that way."

Planning to start his new enterprise properly, Anthony renovated the building complex prior to opening.

"I committed a sin when I got the place," he laughs. "I remodeled! Nobody did that here because the bankers in Savannah didn't want to have anything to do with Tybee at the time" and it was only because of his reputation in the insurance business that bankers agreed to give him a loan.

He says the rarity of renovations on the island was dramatically illustrated when his daughter came home from school one day just after work began on his new establishment.

"She asked, 'Daddy are we in the Mafia?' When I asked where she got that from, she said the kids at school said their parents had told them we were in the Mafia, with us spending all that money remodeling and all!"

"I told her no honey, the Mafia wouldn't even claim us. We can't afford to join up."

His new establishment became what Anthony describes as "a swinging nightclub called The Black Lace Lounge," and the adjacent Deck Motel.

"We brought in professional entertainers for the first time in Chatham County," featuring belly dancers, go-go girls, strippers, female impersonators, and comedians, he says.

"It was always packed. It was a real showplace! We brought in a lot of doctors and lawyers, and we were very strict if you had too much to drink on the job. We did it right."

"And we had everything you can think of, special iridescent lighting and costumes, everything. I had a lot of fun doing that, but I was a lot younger then."

Anthony's high opinion of his operation was confirmed when his Black Lace Lounge was acclaimed as the "Number One Club on the East Coast."

After his success with the lounge, Anthony opened a Ramada Inn, the first national chain motel on the island, where the Econo Lodge now operates. (Tybee's Days Inn was built about the same time as an independent motel, before becoming the first in the Days Inn chain.)

The new motel required so much of his time that Anthony leased the lounge, then closed it down and opened Cap'n Chris Restaurant and Happy Holiday Motel after his lounge business deteriorated under a succession of unsuccessful operators.

Along the way, he has also built townhouses and a warehouse on the island, and in 1995 "I conned him (his son, Chris) into building the Howard Johnson's hotel" across the street from the restaurant, says Anthony, who served as the contractor for the hotel.

"I missed my calling," he says. "I always liked to build."

His daughter, Paula, manages the hotel.

Anthony displays awards won by new hotel he claims he conned his son into building.

Anthony shouldered more than his heavy entrepreneurial load during his early years on the island.

He became active in the Chamber of Commerce and was named its president for three terms, pushing to promote the island as hard as he did his own establishments.

Anthony helped initiate gala Fourth of July celebrations at the beach, as well as a formal parade, unlike the current rolling water fight known as the Beach Bum Parade.

His parade, like the Bums' affair now does, opened the Tybee tourist season, but Anthony dubbed it the "Spring Festival" because "we don't close," he told folks at the time.

"Ours was a real parade," he says. "We had the sheriff's posse and Shriners and high school bands from all over. You had to plan it a year in advance and I put a lot of work into the parade."

His Fourth of July celebration featured not only fireworks but pole climbing contests, greased pig chasing, potato sack races, and watermelon and pie eating contests, "and the beach front was packed all the way down," he recalls.

He also helped bring the first Georgia State Open Surfing Championship to the beach, signing up professional judges for the event, and "we brought in people from California and all over the world" for the competition, says Anthony.

He even played a pivotal role in establishing a Miss Savannah Beach Beauty Pageant before the city's name was formally changed to Tybee Island.

"We put together a nice beauty pageant," he says. "It had three different levels for different ages. We had people register from all over. We put it on first class and had well-known people as judges. It was an outstanding success."

"We put on fishing tournaments too, giving rods and reels and things like that as prizes. We were always doing something. We even started Oktoberfest to bring in people."

"I don't know why they didn't keep up with those things. They just let it all die."

While lots of things have come and gone since Anthony's arrival on the island, growth has surged in both the business and residential sectors, and those who want to build on Tybee no longer have to cajole Savannah bankers to process their loans.

One major breakthrough in that area may be due in large part to Anthony, who headed the island's zoning board of appeals for eight years.

"We helped get the Savannah Beach and Racquet Club," he says. "After that, for the first time the city didn't have to go to the bank in Savannah every winter to borrow money."

"We insisted on their running all their lines for all their services in addition to paying all the fees, and Tybee was in the black."

Anthony encouraged cluster development because "the more you spread 'em out, the more it will cost to provide city services, is what I told 'em. You stack 'em. You stack 'em up like sardines and you have only one line coming in."

"I said stack them Yankees up like sardines and let's enjoy what we've got! I still think that's the way to go."

He also believes the city should do more to encourage businesses "and give them moral support" because the business community provides most of the city's money.

"The last time I asked the mayor, he told me businesses

supplied about 70 percent of Tybee's budget money, and the budget runs $5 million a year now," he says.

"Government costs a lot more than it used to, and it is business that makes it possible. There are a lot of older people on fixed incomes here, and if it weren't for the money businesses bring in, their costs would go up and many would have to leave."

Anthony also has strong feelings about the Tybee's 35-foot building height limitations.

"Just like the design of the roof, for God's sake!" he says. "Why would I want to impose on somebody for four or five more feet to have a flat roof when they could have a nice design? What the heck difference does five or ten more feet make?"

"I don't agree with that philosophy that they're going to block somebody that's 10 blocks back from seeing the ocean. I just don't comprehend that. It doesn't make sense. If you want a view of the ocean, buy beachfront property."

Anthony put this belief into practice as head of Tybee's zoning appeals board when a resident whose home was set back from the beach asked the board to refuse a permit for the owner of the property in front of him to build a house because it would obstruct his view.

"I asked him why he didn't buy the property if he wanted that view since the lot had been on the market for a long time," says Anthony, and when the back lot owner had no reply the building permit was granted.

Anthony stands beside son Chris, seated in a booth in his restaurant.

Despite ongoing controversy about building heights and other problems, however, Anthony says:

"We have a lot of wonderful, conscientious residents down here who are concerned about beautification. By and large they're really dedicated, and everybody has a right to their own opinions. I like where it's going. It looks better now than it ever has."

In response to complaints about the deluge of new condominiums, he says they play a major role in supporting the island for everyone.

"That condominium that Mike Ryan put up (on Strand Avenue) is valued at five or six million dollars for property tax purposes, and it replaced stuff valued at $100,000 or $150,000," says Anthony, "and look at the Ocean Plaza and what it means."

He says he enjoys watching the progress and has always been a big supporter of the island and its people.

Looking around Cap'n Chris Restaurant, Anthony says he figures he'll continue to work with his son "until I die. It's a hard business. You only make money a few months a year, and you try to keep the help year round. Chris needs all the cheap help he can get."

POSTSCRIPT: Cap'n Chris Restaurant and the adjacent motel were sold and razed shortly after this was written. Anthony Pete Simon, who was listed in "Who's Who in Georgia," was 80 when he passed away on July 15, 2007.

Pat Locklear -

Old Warrior Still Fighting for Tybee

Former Mayor Wants Best For Island

He's spent his entire working life serving in public schools, the military and local government, and is now ready to hang it up... almost.

Former Tybee Island Mayor James P. (Pat) Locklear vows that his recent unsuccessful bid for re-election will be his last run for public office.

The feisty, bespectacled former mayor, whose eyes sparkle beneath his curly salt-and-pepper gray hair when he discusses island politics, has some physical problems - he's being treated for a worrisome pancreatic ailment - and says he needs a rest.

But mostly, he says, "I'd almost forgotten how to smile" because of the intense approach he took to both public service in recent years, and the fact that he's long overdue in spending quality time with his family.

Now comfortable with his decision to abandon politics, Pat says he has quickly re-learned the joy of smiling.

He glows with pride and smiles frequently when discussing his adopted son, Michael, who is also his grandson.

"I never had the chance to watch my children (a son and daughter) grow up because I was always away in the service," he says. "I just looked up one day and they were grown. Now I have the time to spend with Michael and it's wonderful, and I'm finally able to have time with Mary (his wife of 40 years). It's great!"

A native of Tybee, Pat, who was given that name because he was born on St. Patrick's Day, had a long and successful run, and his friends agree that he deserves to slow down, though many suspect he won't.

He'll turn 62 in March.

A driving force behind the rejuvenation of both the Tybee Arts Association and Boy Scouts on the island, he has been immersed in community service for years, in addition to serving two terms as a city councilman and one as mayor.

Pat is especially proud of his eight-year-long affiliation with the Boy Scouts.

"We've had three Eagle Scouts" in that time, he says proudly. "Perry Solomon V was the first Tybee Boy Scout in more than 50 years to reach the level of Eagle."

Solomon's grandfather, Perry Solomon III, was Tybee's only previous Eagle Scout, a half century earlier.

Pat has also played a pivotal role in promoting recreation on the island.

During his first city council term he headed a recreation committee and has worked to improve facilities and activities in this area ever since.

Pat's parents (his father was a career soldier assigned to the Medical Corps and his mother a nurse) moved to Tybee in 1931, and the future mayor spent his childhood on the island.

He attended grade school in a small wooden schoolhouse once located on the site of the ball field in Memorial Park and got his first exposure to City Hall when courses were taught in its auditorium as the school's enrollment grew.

Pat graduated from high school at Georgia Military Academy in College Park, which he attended while planning to follow in his father's footsteps, then went to Georgia Tech.

"It took me five years to finish Tech," he laughs. "My freshman year was a disaster. I spent a lot of time partying" after the strict regimen at GMA. "Then I realized I wasn't at Georgia, I was at Georgia Tech, so I had to study."

Pat met his future wife on Tybee during the summer following his GMA graduation, when Mary came up from Tampa to work with her mother taking care of children at the Fresh Air Home.

"Mary and I just hit it off immediately," he says.

They dated steadily through their school years whenever they could arrange to see one another.

About the time he was finishing Tech, Pat asked Mary

to meet him on the beach at the south end of the island, and it was there that he proposed and presented her with the engagement ring.

They were married in the summer of 1958 and settled down to teach in Savannah, Pat at Jenkins, Mary at Eli Whitney Elementary School.

That lasted only a couple of months because Pat, a member of the ROTC in college, volunteered for service and was ordered to attend a school for commissioned officers at Fort Sam Houston.

"We just threw everything we had in the back of our car and headed for Texas," he recalls.

Early in his military career, Pat was ordered to Alabama during the 1960s Birmingham race riots.

"It was interesting," he recalls. "We (Pat and a contingent of his men) left at night to go to Fort McClellan, and when we stopped at a grocery store in Alabama, they slammed the door in our face.

"That's how the people in Alabama felt about us. They did not like federal troops, but that just made us try to do a better job."

He feels fortunate that his unit was never required to enter the fray in Birmingham.

Pat served two tours of duty in Vietnam, before, between, and after which he and Mary traveled throughout the United States and Europe. They spent a total of 12 years in Germany, during which time he rose to the rank of colonel.

Other than Vietnam, Pat says his toughest assignments were at the Pentagon and in Germany, where he served during the latter stages of Vietnam War.

"Everything was being done by committee in Germany since all the noncoms and lieutenants had been shipped to Vietnam," he recalls, noting that there was virtually no discipline among the troops and drug use was rampant.

"You remember McNamara said we weren't drawing down any of the troops in Germany? Well, that was a bald-faced lie!"

Pat was assigned the herculean task of eliminating the use of drugs and instilling order and got a quick introduction to the extent of the problem when he arrived at his base.

"The gate guard had a needle in his arm when I arrived," he grimaces. "And it wasn't like state-side, where you could give your boys a weekend off and send them home to mama. You had to deal with them there."

Early in his assignment, Pat and a fellow officer entered a barracks surprising six soldiers who were preparing to shoot up on drugs.

The biggest man in the group had elastic strapped around his arm and was boiling drugs on a piece of glass. He lunged at Pat with the glass while his cohorts jumped out of the second-floor windows.

Pat, who weighed only 105 pounds at the time, evaded the attack, grabbed the man's arm, and pinned him

Pat Locklear with wife Mary and son Michael in their island home.

against the wall while his fellow officer called for security.

By the time the MPs arrived, "the guy just broke down and cried there on my arm," says Pat.

But, at least in this case, there was a happy ending.

The man agreed to undergo counseling and rehabilitation. About a year later, Pat was visiting a field artillery battalion when a solder walked up and said, "Major Locklear, I want to thank you. You saved my life!"

It was the same man who had attacked him in the barracks.

Hundreds of soldiers were thrown out of the Army, and many were imprisoned during the cleanup effort, according to Pat, who says the situation improved perceptibly when the Vietnam War wound down and noncoms and junior officers were re-assigned with the NATO forces in Europe.

He also recalls more positive experiences during his service in Germany.

One involved a detachment of female Army troops that was assigned to his command. While most were placed in support jobs in offices, and other areas, they joined other servicemen for regular extended field exercises digging trenches, sleeping in tents, and operating in a front-line environment with NATO forces which were on constant alert.

"They were regular troops, and they did an outstanding job," he says. "Of the 11 months they were there, we spent nine of them in the field. They took care of themselves, and they worked hard. I was proud to have them under my command."

Pat says he is still perturbed by the political intervention of former Sen. William Proxmire, who insisted that the females be pulled out of the area when he learned they were serving in a combat unit.

"In a combat unit, it's hard to draw a line saying this is the front and that is the rear," says Pat. "It was particularly difficult where we were, facing the Russians. Everything was the front."

He also recalls a large-scale NATO exercise called "Flintlock" with justifiable pride.

Pat's battalion was assigned to simulate "the bad guys" in control of a designated area.

Special Forces units from 11 different countries were arrayed against them, and many of those highly trained troops parachuted into nearby mountains to swoop down on Pat's soldiers.

"My boys did a real good job," he says. "We captured the entire Norwegian contingent, including the commander. We had them on the run so long they hadn't eaten in days."

"We also scattered the French, and the Greeks were never able to get off the mountain. We had a good time, but the Special Forces weren't very happy. The opposition commander said his group had never been beaten so badly."

Pat's final military assignment was at the Pentagon.

"It was the last place I wanted to be after seeing that parking lot (with its endless rows of thousands of cars)," he says.

Pat was an assistant desk officer in the office of the secretary of defense, and "that's where I got to watch real politicians work," says Pat.

He remained in his position through the Ford and Carter administrations, handling the high-profile German desk under Carter.

Pat says he kept two secretaries busy and would sometimes work until after midnight drawing up plans to conform to the direction Carter outlined.

"The next morning Carter would change his mind 180 degrees, and the plans had to be scrapped and new ones drawn up," he says. "We had a hard time keeping up with what the President wanted for policy. It was difficult and frustrating."

"The one constant was the bureaucracy. The bureaucrats stayed on when administrations changed. They're the ones who were running the place, and you really don't want them running anything. You need leadership from the top."

"You talk about points of light! With bureaucrats you get 360 degrees worth of light points."

Pat had the opportunity to remain in Washington, but says he was disenchanted with the machinations inside the Beltway, was burned out after 10 years of Pentagon service, and opted for retirement after 23 years in the infantry.

When he returned to his home on Tybee for his "retirement," Pat hit the island running and became involved in a myriad of activities.

In addition to his work with the Arts Association and Boy Scouts, he is president of the Optimist Club and was active in the overall island youth program.

Then he was surprised to find himself running for public office.

"I have no idea how it happened," he says. "I wasn't interested in politics at all. I guess it grew out of my volunteer work. But I did enjoy it when I got in there."

That enjoyment did not come immediately, however. Pat won his first term on council in an unofficial grouping with Mayor Charles Hosti and Jeff Dukes, another new city councilman.

His introduction to the serious nature of Tybee politics came several days after that victory when a disgruntled islander threw a stone through his bedroom window.

The culprit was the same person who had just smashed the rear window of Hosti's truck and was headed over to Dukes' house when Pat called the police.

Authorities were never able to identify, let alone capture, the offender.

After a second term on council, Pat was elected mayor, then sat out a term when he was defeated by Mayor Walter Parker in the 1995 election.

He was particularly perturbed by that defeat because he felt he had a lot of work left to be done.

"I focused on the infrastructure," he says. "Beach renourishment is important, and you can't drop the ball on that, but it's a problem for the state."

"The sewer lines and water lines on Tybee are absolutely disastrous. A brand-new school bus fell in a hole at Jones and Second Avenue, and they just pulled it out and filled in behind it. It's still collapsing over there. If you can't see it, they don't fix it."

"What I wanted was a $3 million water and sewer bond issue to take care of water, sewer, and storm drains, and council gave me a $2 million bond issue. With that money we filled all the main water lines going south and used some of the money to take care of some sewer problems."

"That's the one thing I left. I started that. It needs to be continued. It hasn't been followed through with as much as it should. The elected terms ought to be for four years. You simply can't accomplish enough with only two years in office."

Pat and Michael.

Pat believes the failing infrastructure is still the island's biggest problem and is especially concerned about the sewer system.

"It's going to be a real problem during the tourist season, and the fine for going over capacity (in drawing water from the aquifer) is tremendous. Fines could be $25,000 a day."

"I'm afraid if we keep going the way we are going, we're not going to have enough money to take care of our problems, and we may lose our charter."

"Tybee and Spanish Hammock use more water per capita than any other area in the county, and something has to be done to address the problem."

He was negotiating with Fort Stewart officials to arrange for Tybee to obtain part of the fort's water allocation, but says his plan was not pursued when he left office.

Pat remains intensely interested in island improvement and says he wants to help promote the redesign of the business area along Tybrisa Street, several plans for which were recently submitted by SCAD students.

"I'll do anything I can to help Tybee to be a better place to live," he says. "I've been a lot of places in the world, and I've found none better."

He is particularly enthusiastic when he reflects on the sunshine days of his youth on Tybee "when it was the place we all like to remember."

"It was beautiful then. Most of this (the area around his home on the north side of Highway 80 at Miller Avenue) was all sand dunes. There were all sorts of places to play, and only about 600 people lived on the island."

"We would sit on our porch and identify the cars. Back in those days there were only a few different makes, and maybe in an hour we'd have two or three pass."

"And our parents gave us free rein. We'd go to the beach and take our dogs with us. We'd go crabbing, wearing shoes in the water, and just reach down and grab the crabs, there were so many of them. We'd throw them in big drums near the water."

He also recalls skating on the old pier and the fun times he had hanging out at the bowling alley.

"And you could go horseback riding," he recalls, noting that his father used to ride with Col. George C. Marshall Jr., who was commander at Fort Screven at the time.

Pat says he was saddened when he returned to the island after retirement to learn that horses were no longer allowed within the city limits.

"Nobody got in trouble in those days," he says. "There was only one police officer on Tybee. He was a tall man, about 6-foot-3, who we used to call 'High Pockets.' There was no jail, and if you made a mistake, you paid for it right there."

Pat says he wants to ensure his son has similar memories about growing up on the island and savors every moment he shares with the boy as he grows.

Pat is an old warrior come home, where he plans to continue fighting to make Tybee a better place for all of us.

POSTSCRIPT: Pat Locklear got what he hoped for regarding those two-year terms for Tybee's mayor and city council members not long after he stepped down from an active role in politics. The city increased council's terms to four years, thus enabling many projects to be completed before elections rolled around again. Pat was honored with the passage by the Georgia House of Representatives of Resolution 611 "for his illustrious and selfless service to our nation and his lifetime of faithful service to his community and his many contributions for Georgia." He and his wife Mary continue to live a well deserved, very relaxed life on Tybee.

Linda Lindeborg -

Artist Taking Talent to Larger Venue

Dreams of Making Her Mark With Atlanta Studio

Linda Lindeborg

She's at the top of the food chain in Tybee Island's highly active art community but feels this is akin to being a big fish in a relatively small pond.

Artist Linda Lindeborg, who creates, displays, and sells her work in the Nautilus Studio beside Highway 80, believes she has reached that stage in life where she must fish or cut bait, and she's opting for the former, far from the waters surrounding Tybee, to see just how far her artistic abilities will carry her.

She says she has the opportunity for the first time to embark on "a really positive way to get known, to go up to another level" by having another person "dedicated to marketing my work who has as much to gain by making me collectable as I do."

Linda plans to move her art into a new fine art gallery just north of Atlanta where she will be the "keystone artist."

"One of the main reasons I am making this leap now

is that I am 58, and I know that if I don't try this, I'm going to look back in eight or ten years and say I wonder what I could have done," she says.

The marketing end of her art will be turned over to her daughter, Vanessa, who is preparing to open the new gallery.

"She will be highly motivated because she is going to inherit every bit of copyright I own, so it's a financial carrot and an emotional one too for her," according to Linda, who says many artists "who have become household names" have followed this route.

She says the wives of nationally known artist Ray Ellis, who has a studio in Savannah, and Andrew Wyeth, handle their marketing, noting:

"They have had the pure luxury of saying you go sell it, I'm going to paint. Their marketers are not just motivated by that long-term residual."

This will be true of her daughter as well, she says, "because whatever Vanessa ends up inheriting from me, the value is going to be in my collectability as an artist. She has the opportunity to have an effect on me."

Linda plans to sell her island studio and home and move to the Duluth, Georgia area where her daughter expects to open the new gallery in October.

It will be called "vboggs galleries," offering collectable art as well as collectable wine (Vanessa is also an authority on wines, according to her mother), and will include a wine tasting area featuring north Georgia vineyards.

Linda Lindeborg smiles while recalling her grandfather.

Vanessa will represent several regional artists, including three from Savannah, but "it will be mainly, mainly my work," Linda says. "When this gallery opens, she will be the fourth generation in my family in the arts."

Linda's father was an artist/craftsman who worked mostly in wood. It was her grandfather, a water colorist in Ohio and California, who first sparked her interest in art at age 4. She became fixated on his paintings and pestered him to let her into his studio.

"I was fascinated by the whole idea of his art studio and the smell," she recalls. "To this day when I open linseed oil, it's like a rush and my grandfather's there."

"He started teaching me, but he taught me first to see. He'd walk me through things and say look at this and look at the shape, feel the shape."

"He said your mind is going to tell you that the bottom of a cup is flat because it sits on a flat table and it doesn't rock, but stand over it and you'll find the bottom is round."

She describes her grandfather as fascinating, not only because of his art, for which he was highly regarded late in life when he retired to California, but because of his early success as an entrepreneur, and his unusual marriage.

While still in his late 20s, he owned and operated one of the first Standard Oil of Ohio filling stations, and married an Amish girl he met in Pennsylvania while painting there one summer.

Her grandmother was just 17 when she ran away from her family's devout Amish compound to marry him.

Two of Linda's treasured keepsakes are the Amish doughboy her grandmother brought with her and a large watercolor of a forest scene painted by her grandfather in 1913. She plans to pass the painting to her daughter on its hundredth birthday.

Linda studied with her grandfather until she was 9, when her parents enrolled her in an art institute near their Zanesville, Ohio home.

"I had a fabulous teacher at the art institute, and when I got to high school, he was the head of the art department," she says. "He was like a mentor."

Linda feels extremely lucky because "I knew from the time I was little being an artist was what I wanted and it's still a thrill to me. A lot of people never really know what they want to be. They grow up, and they go to school and then fall into something."

An only child, she says she was always a real tomboy, noting:

"There were 28 of us on my mother's side...first cousins. Twenty-four of them were boys, and it was like having a lot of brothers. I grew very comfortable in the company of men and still feel they are more honest and infinitely kinder" than women.

"I was always outside. I had this marvelous tricycle. The handlebars were lined all the way around with squirrel tails. My dad would hunt and I would get the trophies."

"I was raised as a boy, a little differently. Dad taught me all about the earth, pretty much a pagan way of living."

Those lessons are reflected in both her life and art.

"I still mark the trines (aspects of 120 degrees, give or take 6 or 8 degrees, usually occurring between signs sharing the same elements, such as fire and earth), she says.

"I mark the solstice. I mark the equinox. My paintings reflect the equality of things, which is very important."

She says her art depicting spring has an equal amount of light and dark "because that's that time. The very, very light ones are going to be summer.

Linda looks forward to bigger things.

It's just in me. It's what I am."

Linda attended Madison College in Virginia, where she earned her bachelor's degree in studio arts before earning a degree in graphic design and illustration from the Art Institute of Pittsburg.

Then she moved to Nashville to begin what would be a career of more than 20 years doing illustrations for print media, along with architectural renderings for a company she operated with her first husband.

Linda discusses her art.

After their marriage went south, Linda did too, heading for Atlanta where she worked as studio director for a large advertising agency while creating illustrations for magazines.

With the contacts she made there and at a subsequent position with a large association, she continued her commercial artwork on a freelance basis.

About ten years ago she decided to dedicate her time to her real love, fine art.

Linda admits her decision was a gigantic leap of faith, given the lucrative nature of her commercial artwork, but says within four years she was making more money in fine art than she did in her previous career as an illustrator.

"I've been very fortunate," she smiles. "My work sells."

Linda produces around 30 paintings a year, most of which are sold to art lovers visiting her studio even before she completes them.

In addition to these, she does a flourishing business in prints of her originals, selling them wholesale to franchise art dealers.

When she first arrived on Tybee, Linda was known as the "Lighthouse Artist" because of her numerous paintings of the Tybee Lighthouse.

Her work was an instant hit but "to me, that's not art," she says in retrospect. "That's an illustration of a lighthouse, but that's what people want, and I can't forget I am painting for a public."

"We laugh about blue skies and white puffy clouds, and I have done other than that, but people just love the ones with the blue skies and white puffy clouds."

Linda believes the patrons of an artist have specific expectations about their work and are put off by any dramatic change.

"I do a lot of stuff that never gets shown here," she says. "I do a lot of big abstract work, and I don't even bother showing it here because I know what the reaction would be: 'That doesn't look like something you did'."

She has used a pseudonym, Claire Robertson, on some of this work, which was sold through a corporate representative to large businesses.

"The people who bought it didn't care about the name," she says. "They weren't buying collectable art. They were buying stuff for their offices, and I was doing it for the money. I was matching surface swatches."

But Linda insists on reserving some of her time for what she considers more meaningful work which, while it may have no commercial value, could take her to an entirely new level in lucrative painting.

"I am in the planning stages of a series called Beneath," she says. "I've been wanting to do it for about two years."

"I love trees, the structure of trees and everything about them. I've got all the sketches done. None of the paintings are finished."

Her realistic paintings of trees will cover eight panels.

None will be of an entire tree, with most showing just the trunk or base.

"As the tree comes to the ground, things become abstracted and go beneath," she says. "There's a lot of symbolism and mythology involved" like that reflected in the myth about "Merlin being captured by the women of Avalon and buried and kept captive beneath an oak tree."

"I have no idea whether these things will be commercially viable, and I don't care."

"I think this is my opportunity to go to a different venue, a much larger venue. People with a whole lot more money who are interested in spending it on their homes and on art, to give them something a little bit different. I'm really excited about it."

"I'm hoping that they're going to be critically successful even if they're not financially successful. That would be more important to me now at this phase I'm in."

Linda says she doesn't "really have to worry about sales" because she has a large inventory of fine reproductions with a ready market.

"I really feel like there's always going to be a market for high quality stuff," she says, but she also believes there will continue to be a market for "local art, especially in a place like this (Tybee) where people come to visit, and they just want to take a little bit home with them and they look for local art, and that's a good thing."

"Local art is a definite genre, and it has a place in the scheme of things. A lot of residents have retired from some other thing and have decided to be an artist."

Despite their lack of fame "there's a satisfaction level, and that's what it's all about. It's all coming from the inside anyway."

"It is really kind of silly to put a hierarchy on things" because "beauty is in the eye of the beholder."

Linda feels some island artists might have made it big had they really wanted to.

She singles out Sally Bostwick, who she refers to as "the grand dame of beach art."

"I think Sally is fabulous. I consider Sally to be a very fine artist."

"I don't know that she has ever even attempted to get in a gallery in Atlanta. She probably hasn't. She couldn't care less, probably. She sells everything she does."

"She is at the top of her game in that genre, and nobody can do it better. I hope I live long enough to paint a sand dune as well as that woman, and the fact that she never became known regionally or nationally is just due to the fact that that's what she wanted, or maybe she just was not afforded the opportunity."

"She could have. There's no question about it."

As to her own art, Linda says "my advantage has been in composition because I was trained as a graphic designer. My training went to the heart of inviting a

Linda's Tybee art studio.

reader or viewer to see on a printed page exactly what you wanted them to see."

"I use these same elements in fine art, all of those things to bring your eye in and move it around the page to make sure you see the picture of the product, what it was all about. I use it every day."

Linda will take the reputation and skills she has developed as a fine artist on Tybee to the larger art scene in Atlanta immediately after selling her studio/home on the island but says she will always maintain her affection for Tybee and hopes to return for frequent visits.

Look out world, here she comes!

POSTSCRIPT: Linda sold her Tybee studio and

moved to Atlanta with husband Rik. Her paintings were displayed at "vboggs Gallery," operated by her daughter Vanessa in Suwanee, just outside Atlanta, until the gallery was sold several years ago. Linda gave her grandfather's 1913 painting to Vanessa on its 100th anniversary in 2013. She completed her "Beneath" project, which turned out to be ten, rather than eight panels, and each sold quickly as individual paintings. Along the way she was commissioned to do a painting of Ft. Pulaski on an ornament for the White House Christmas tree and was selected as one of 12 artists to paint scenes of iconic spots in Georgia for a video series on Georgia Public Television. Linda says she has achieved everything she hoped for in terms of recognition and monetary rewards "and then some", and now spends much of her time visiting her grandchildren. "Now I paint only what I want and I don't try or need to sell anything," she says. Rik, who was a highly successful inventor and businessman, passed away after an extended illness the morning following the winter solstice on Dec. 22, 2017, just days after he promised he would remain with her until daylight began to lengthen after the solstice. Linda says at 10 p.m. on the following year's winter solstice, she sat quietly thinking of Rik when she was enveloped by the distinct aroma of his cologne "and I knew he was there." She has performed the same ritual every year since his passing.

Appendix

The articles in this volume were originally published in the Savannah Morning News. The original publication dates for each are as follows:

1. Basil Jackson 12/1/2005
2. Carl Looper..9/16/1998
3. Olivera Lee 3/11/1999
4. Cullen Chambers 1/17/1997
5. Dale Williams and Debbie Kearney....6/18/1998
6. Bonnie Gaster 2/5/1998
7. Freddie Grotheer 3/13/1998
8. Espy Geissler 8/7/1996
9. Debbie Brady Robinson 3/19/1998
10. Ed Towns...4/16/1998
11. Jodee Sadowsky 5/27/1999
12. Robin Arnsdorff 4/2/1998
13. Jack Youmans 9/26/1996
14. Spec Hosti 8/8/1996
15. Judy Helmey 1/10/1997
16. Joe Jackson 2/26/1997
17. Mallory Pearce 3/1/1999
18. Kathryn Williams 9/29/1996
19. Mike Scarbrough.................................4/28/2006
20. Charlie Sherrill 3/26/1997
21. Maria Rodriguez 4/29/1999
22. Anthony Simon 3/26/1998
23. Pat Locklear 1/22/1998
24. Linda Lindeborg 8/11/2006

Acknowledgements

I am indebted to a number of people who played an instrumental role helping me make this book a reality.

I'm especially grateful to Mallory Pearce, the noted Tybee ecologist, artist, calligrapher and author, for creating caricatures of each of the book's characters and to my long-time friend Suzi Fuchs, a former journalist and public relations specialist, for her early editing assistance.

My thanks go out as well to newspaper columnist and author Ben Goggins for his final editing, sound advice and consistent encouragement, and to layout designer Lauren Clackum, known fondly as the "Princess of Pages," for her outstanding craftsmanship in formatting and design.

Both Miranda Carter and Nita Martin have my gratitude for saving me substantial time and effort by re-typing columns from old newspapers which had not been preserved in my computer files.

A final thanks goes to my sister, Jackie Eggerton, for her excellent proofreading which caught a number of errors the rest of us missed, as well as to the many friends who encouraged me to continue working on this project.

Without each of you, along with the wonderful, idiosyncratic folks who I have come to know on Tybee, this book would never have been possible.

Coming Soon

Even More TYBEE ISLAND *HEROES AND HOOLIGANS*

The Making of an Island Paradise, Vol. 3

www.ingramcontent.com/pod-product-compliance
Lightning Source LLC
Chambersburg PA
CBHW071400200726
48294CB00004B/1234

* 9 7 8 1 9 5 9 5 6 3 0 8 2 *